PENNYWEIGHT WINDOWS

ALSO BY DONALD REVELL

From the Abandoned Cities

The Gaza of Winter

New Dark Ages

Erasures

Beautiful Shirt

Alcools (translation)

There Are Three

Arcady

My Mojave

The Self-Dismembered Man (translation)

Invisible Green: Selected Prose

PENNYWEIGHT WINDOWS

New & Selected Poems   DONALD REVELL

Alice James Books • FARMINGTON, MAINE

10 9 8 7 6 5 4 3 2 1

Alice James Books are published by Alice James Poetry
Cooperative, Inc., an affiliate of the University of Maine at Farmington.

ALICE JAMES BOOKS
238 Main Street
Farmington, ME 04938

www.alicejamesbooks.org

LIBRARY OF CONGRESS CATALOGING-IN-PUBLICATION DATA
Revell, Donald, 1954–
Pennyweight windows : new & selected poems / Donald Revell.
    p.   cm.
ISBN 1–882295–51–x — ISBN 1–882295–52–8 (pbk.)
I. Title.
PS3568.E793P46 2005
811'.54—dc22   2004026191

Alice James Book gratefully acknowledges support from the University of Maine at
Farmington and the National Endowment for the Arts. ❧

COVER IMAGE: Edouard Vuillard: "Les deux écoliers" (Inv. 6681, Ekta MV057).
Musées royaux des Beaux-Arts de Belgique, Bruxelles - Koninklijke Musea voor
Schone Kunsten van België, Brussel. (photo Speltdoorn, 9 x 12).

For my mother

DORIS REVELL,

and in memory of my father

DONALD REVELL, SR. (1918-1995)

Youth supplies us with colors age with canvass.
How rare it must be that in age our life
receives a new coloring. The heavens were blue
when I was young and that is their color still.
Paint is costly . . . I think the heavens have
had but one coat of paint since I was a boy.
And their blue is paled & dingy & worn off
in many places. I cannot afford to give them
another coat—Where is the man so rich that
he can give the earth a second coat of green in
his manhood—or the heavens a second coat
of blue. Our paints are all mixed when we are
young. Methinks the skies need a new coat.
Have our eyes any blue to spare?

—HENRY DAVID THOREAU

Journal, January 26, 1852

CONTENTS

FROM *Arcady*

FROM *My Mojave*

New Poems

ACKNOWLEDGEMENTS

Grateful acknowledgment is made for permission to reprint poems from the following books:

From the Abandoned Cities. Copyright © 1983 by Donald Revell. Reprinted with the permission of HarperCollins Publishers.
The Gaza of Winter. Copyright © 1988 by Donald Revell. Reprinted with the permission of The University of Georgia Press.
New Dark Ages. Copyright © 1990 by Donald Revell. Reprinted with the permission of Wesleyan University Press.
Erasures. Copyright © 1992 by Donald Revell. Reprinted with the permission of Wesleyan University Press.
Beautiful Shirt. Copyright © 1994 by Donald Revell. Reprinted with the permission of Wesleyan University Press.
There Are Three. Copyright © 1998 by Donald Revell. Reprinted with the permission of Wesleyan University Press.
Arcady. Copyright © 2002 by Donald Revell. Reprinted with the permission of Wesleyan University Press.

Some poems from the "New Poems" section of this volume originally appeared in the following periodicals, whose editors the author wishes to thank: *American Poetry Review, Barrow Street, The Canary, Conjunctions, Denver Quarterly, Kiosk, Mississippi Review, Pequod,* and *Slope.*

The following poems also appeared in a chapbook entitled *Revival House,* published by *Rain Taxi*. Many thanks to the editors. "Visions of the Daughters of Albion: A Screenplay," "My Virtuous Pagan," "Vietnam Epic Treatment," "The Bishop's Wife," "A Green Hill Far Away," and "The Celandine Creed."

FROM

From the Abandoned Cities

Central Park South

The way the buildings curve (as if a thought
or big dream you could never really get
your brain to go about fixing for you, had
for once become a grand hotel, an all-
forgiving gray exterior like that
which faces north across the park and loves
you) makes you think of any afternoon
at five in late October and of how
the girl you followed used to disappear
into the Plaza. Nothing has changed along
that street. You walk. You watch a limousine
go by. You look for actresses. The light
is still what you remember having thought of
when you thought of Venice, Henry James,
or being happy—blue, with a touch of gray
and orange. Only your nerves can rot; the rest
goes on discriminating, particularly
places. There have always been those places,
real corners that can stay there and forgive your
wanting a drink or having once believed
that love should be conducted openly
and in the daytime. If you could wrap your mind
around the park, the way these walls do, you
would rot a little more slowly. Maybe if
you dreamed the way a building dreams
you might even heal. Remembering that girl
was not a bad way to start. Just follow her
along the park side now, but go west, away
from that hotel that always put an end
to everything. At Columbus, turn and head
for the museum where they put the bones
together; you'll be glad of bones by then
or, with a bit of luck, side by side
with the girl, having forgotten. Either way,
romantic Venice is alive in New York
again. The lights are as blue as ever; the park
is colorful at night, in October.

What you came for were the curves. You got them.
Look at how the buildings curve around and close in
lovingly. You'd been following love then.
Now it is a street beside the park.

Belfast

Go north any way and sadness clings to the ground
like fog. The sound of voices goes wrong and can't
be followed. You hear, you breathe cries with a damp wind.

Go north to the ruined counties where girls chant
over a piece of wood called "Doll-Who's-Dead"
and where the streets you walk are a dead giant

who won't rise. Here, History is the unfed
beast past scaring who comes down from the hills
in daylight. It kills anything, in broad

daylight, then is itself stalked until
the men corner it in some back street. They save
the town for the next beast the granite hills

won't hold. And here, Journey's End is the gray
wall, bled white in patches, that divides
bare yard from bare yard, the unsaved from the unsaved.

In the forlorn business of taking sides,
the rain and the rituals of grief have no
part. Each renews the other as each abides

into the next day's routine, into the slow
recessionals of grief and steady rain.
Here, one death's as just as its counterpart as both

right nothing and are only as wrong as the changes
they were meant but failed to bring about.
Here, suffering betrays itself in exchange

for a dead march, too wise to ever doubt
life has no grander end than a parade
into the next street. The bold dead are borne out

of trouble, brought closer to the sea and laid
down. The living are marched back by pipes to their
reprisals in the bare yards. From either side

of walls that bleed, voices you can't trace rise and tear
the wind into mad gusts. Tomorrow, History
returns. Tonight, the ruined counties prepare.

In Lombardy

She mocks the bones in you, as if it had
been Lombardy you met in, and around
the time of Da Vinci, the man who painted her,
an unboxed body at the center of a sad
procession, womanly, in the veil of a drowned
innocent, and in control. The myrrh,
the acolytes attending, these conjoin
with the figure into an adequate conceit
for what is meant by fear of dying. Her
relationship to the thing is not the point
however, nor is that humiliating street

through which she is attended by the boys
the course of it. Germane to all who swing
the censer, chant, or carry candles are
those inamoratas, those comic angels poised
as if in mockery or blackface, wing
to wing in jibing constellations, stars
in rows. Perfection, the maestro's real intent,
is laughter, alive as its direction toward
the living drowned, the lucky ones. Effect,
a countereffect, and the seduction were all meant
to mock us, to seduce our hearts and record
us, aching in ourselves that way. What was intact

was deformed. There was also that fear's result, and what
love means, considering. It means the blank
regard of one's own feet as they progress
along the assigned paths, recalling those facts,
this dread. It means a failing brain at the brink
of hypnosis, permanently. Being less
and more than that, the woman died to be
an object in the mind's expansion, to appear
expansively as what we desire: a pale
seductress robed in gauze, a fantasy
in black or red or anything as near
a fate like Ruth's amidst strange sheaves. Regale

the visual and be recorded, that
is what the body was to have required
of us. Yet if laughter failed, if what took place
did not amuse the angels nor permit
the minds attending to be so inspired
as to collapse upon themselves, her face
alone might have done it. Having been close
enough, there is, in the death, a single thought
whose mystery is almost comic. In
that, only those accompanying her or those
particular amours whom she had brought
to Lombardy for the occasion, loves

born of another hand's intention, could
take part. The face is beautiful. These men
she mocks, the redundant, particular ones, perform
for her, are the desperately in need and would,
without a doubt, be no impediment
to her complete possession of their more
aesthetic realities, their minds as well
as of their senses. Love, for our
enchanting lady, is an abstracted grove
of familiar symbols where a mind can swell
like music, overcome by its own power
to invent, without compassion and above

regalia. As an event, the woman continues,
is in our eyes, by moments indiscreet
or present, then and now depending on
the mind or eyes of imaging. The tense
deformity, the actual defeat
of Time through her specific love, is bond
and compact, then, and more than likely years
from then, as well as now in Lombardy
or there in Leonardo's picture. Made
by thoughts of death into a living fear
of bodies, we define a landscape. She
records us in it, weeping, nearly mad.

Just Lord

You are that color in the air I love
and myself, and might have saved me. Have I held
on pointlessly, forgetting that hard days live
in you and are returned through nightmare? Hell
is the one dream I cannot give up to you.
If, holding on, I fell, it was my sick
heart kept me living and hating the world's use
of the afflicted for mere color. More pricks
than kicks is their framed adage, and as I read
it now, it has kept faith. There is neither
hope nor love in anyone, is there? Need
is the one good you allow, the one grace, whether
or not we twist it into a wrongful love
of you. I need you. I am yours to make live.

Bal des Ardents

1.

Our deaths, the fires we invite by need,
fit effect to rage. We burn and so are freed

of the anger life becomes after infancy,
of the absurd challenges days deal. That we

are wasted to no end is the light we give
you, for virtue. It completes us. It may survive

us, feed the flames a while longer. The wild act
upheld beyond itself by an effect.

We burn. We run to the screams and back, to white
arms lifted in despair and back. Tonight

concludes an argument we've had with our lives.
In waste, we find the excess excess forgives.

2.

Of what am I but these others? Their
brief violence gives a name to what
I could not name, their obscenity
a rude cause to hopelessness. If what
I am is one of these, dancing, I
am assumed into Death's chivalry.

The others have their hysteria.
Unmoved in the fire, I see as light
sees, through the forms that fail, to that
one emptiness each returns to. White
Hart. Fleur-de-Lys. These others whose cries
are answered by scorn in histories.

3.

It was too horrible to be made up or
embellished. I remember holding out
my arms and stepping back. I called the name
of each that burned as he burned, took one step back
for each. The future ended then, as burnt
leaves rising upon thermals from a fire

end: withered, blackened, insubstantial. What
remained was the poor, poor joke we have for life.
Some nights now I stretch out my arms to nothing,
call the names, and wake into a fear
too absolute to name or to live with. They
died first and horribly. I follow, close.

4.

There is the heat that continues, the bad light.
What an event comes down to is less than these,
as here, now, I can neither hear the screams
shrill, shot through flames, nor mourn anyone. The White

Harts, Fleurs-de-Lys. What emblems can I love
or lose or waken to the dumb regret of
here, where only I am and fear has names?
I read the chronicles that scorn the obscene,

mad boys. Unlike them, like you, I am past wasting.
Excess punishes me, never forgives.
Our deaths, the fires we will fight and lose to,
arrive coolly and last. They complete nothing.

5.

A broken allure keeps history alive.
Seeing it wrecked, innocent, we forgive.

Tokens

With none of the décor then, none
of the loveliness heart freaks for it-
self out of thin air, there is mind
caught scribbling: gaunt designs of what
fear changed or left to stand in white
rooms, as in amber, to cheat life.

It is, I'm certain, the same feeling.

There is also the collapse of life
into signs and tokens. I preserve
these, use the homeliest for comfort—
the woman's face inside a shell,
the white heart in amber. They change fear
into the little designs I love.

It is, I'm certain, the same feeling.

Mignonette

The metaphors are what has really happened. When
the stars go, it's a person going, or an old
religion folding like a lawn chair, only less
dramatic, less whatever you would call a girl
with cancer or a star that fell. The metaphors

are at the convent where she had so many friends,
so many things to talk about, and they are the blue-
green of an ocean, only more like stars. The white
embroidery, her body white and smooth beneath it,
folded in a chair, is wonderful to think of

when the moon's in Cancer. She would dream about
the lawn or of the convent moon where men betray
themselves. A lawn could only think of dreaming. Think
about a girl you saw by moonlight, dancing on
the lawn. You see a window seat from where you see

a chair in which a girl is dying. Cancer kills,
and only stars can help her. Mignonette, the love
of whom is dancing on the lawn like convent stars,
could never have religion, white as she could be
for anyone who talked to her or sat beside her

in the little chair, not even now, with stars
about to fall and cancer. Metaphors are what
a girl depends on at a time like this, because
the way they work is musical, and music makes
you feel good, even if you're not religious. Life

is any convent, any constellation or
a chair to die in, dreaming of the way a lawn
can look. You looked at her again to see
a proof of something, but you didn't find it, didn't
betray yourself. The metaphors are what you said

would happen: stars around a chair; the cancer
of a girl who dances on the lawn and likes to talk
about religion when the moon's up. What you said
is that you dreamed of watching. Music dreamed. The silk,
what is so white around her folded body, watched.

Here to There

The biggest part of any story is rooms
and the things inside them. Everything else is too
vague, too uncertain in the way it happens,
changes or recites the lines it was
created to recite to live on its own.
I have a picture of an old friend naked,
her head tilted into shadow like
an Odalisque's. Whenever I look at it,
I remember first the room that it was taken in,
then her. I see the photograph
of a Brancusi head I'd tacked to the wall
behind her, then hers, tilted into shadow.
That lost room and the tacked-up photograph
keep her alive the way a mirror keeps
a ghost. Their strength is the reality
she uses. Seeing them, I see her live.

Supported by what surrounds it, an event,
even the briefest kind, like some feelings (missing
a park or girl, nostalgia for the brickworks)
or a sudden chill, takes place as an idea
of dumb things whose presence, by
supporting, sponsors it. Whatever happens
originates with them, leads back to them.
Not that my Odalisque was dreamed up by the walls
exactly, nor that missing her I act
out scenes from something that the desk or clock
radio ordered up. It's no occult
Cultural Geography that accounts
for how a life is channeled through its own days,
turned back upon itself for years sometimes,
for no reason, only to conclude as another
usual small tour of familiar rooms.

As in the theater, where stage, props, scenery
pre-exist the action of a play
and outlast it and can bring it back, our rooms,

made into places by the events they've sponsored,
represent the mystery of how
things live and make us live. The origins
of change, they stand still, conduct what enters them.
My friend is what her picture lets her be.
What I remember is what the room, or rather
what that corner of it I can see
keeps. Everything between us returns there
when it returns. Our story, or anything
that happens, happens as the interval
between one stillness and another. Rooms
fix an itinerary of still points
at the two ends of memory and join them.

Homage

I have looked into the air between my hands
and seen the white ovals, the abstracted, green
or blue eyes of maps of cities. Every face

accuses: the wrong of exile; the worse wrong
of pity, which is like the rain on metal
railings or like the sounds at night that fix

themselves to the shadows of small leaves and change
as the wind changes. I even name them sometimes.
Ellen. Madrid. The one whose eyes were too

close to one another, who was called Berthe.
The naming puts them at a distance and down
to where a thing can be fought for, lost, and then

forgotten easily. In the abandoned,
white cities of a republic, the names are eyes
on walls. The rain, if it rains, makes them luminous.

I have looked into the faces between my hands
and seen years fail. The abandoned cities reclaim
themselves for themselves and shine with exile, with pity.

FROM

The Gaza of Winter

Birthplace

Looking for one hand waving out of the shadowbox
of streets, the staggered cars and railings,
lights hesitating between the shifts of wind,

I do not find it. Designed for no one,
no effect in mind, these fronts and disappearing
corners are as dour as they are plainly habitable.

They confine the street fiercely.
They limit it to those unresponding,
defaced versions of itself I cannot change.

A place to be used, impossible really to love
except as a thing survived, a scar.
And what I do not find here confirms more

than the blankness of one street. These metal awnings,
these Virgins tilting beside the failed trees and ashcans,
pronounce the end of an idea: that people,

given the raw materials and time,
will shape a place to their needs, will lift it up
along the bright curve of their shared, best hopes.

The people here hoped only to stay on.
Taught only to arrive, to get this far
and no farther, they could not imagine

any use in altering a haven that worked
so well it buried them. Between the shifts of wind,
they are proved right, and I do not exist.

The Children's Undercroft

In rooms beneath the church, we stood up singing.
We marched behind our little cross in time
to the yellow keys of someone's cast-off spinet,
wishing we were upstairs under the big cross.
The light was ordinary as it fell in
through plain windows near the ceiling.
We kept thinking of the adults and of *their* windows—
angels and doves in blood-red clouds. We marched
and waited to march up to the real kingdom.

If there are many mansions, there are many
rooms, surely. The ones I'm thinking of now
were a brown cluster of alcoves named for whatever
child saint, crowned and smiling under its cracked
bell jar, each contained. We were assigned
to alcoves by grades. After the hymns and marching,
we would gather around our saints in folding chairs
and learn to be just like them, to merit, like them,
an eternity of crowned, famous smiling.

It was a lesson that would not end, even
when we had folded up our chairs and stacked them
in the last ritual of our small Sunday.
Perfection, fame, and an ecstatic death
seemed all of a piece. Anything less, anything
as stained and usual as our own lives,
was an impoverishment we could not imagine
and had to live with anyway. It would drag
through unremarkable events towards nothing

happy. For us, as we stood waiting
among the crooked stones of the churchyard to be taken
home, eternity would either come soon
or in time only to be more of the same
anxious, unecstatic marching.
Every Sunday, the spinet would sound more
cast-off. Our easy hymns would become dull
or silly. Over-rehearsed, we would at last
enter the real kingdom unmoved and not sing.

The More Lustrous

So many things arrive as themselves and need
no witnesses. Complete under the fretted,
bronze glare of city nights or in the sudden
flat light of the country, they are already
beyond us. They are unvarying, and as
they appear, we break ourselves to pieces against them.

One time, Central Park was covered in new snow,
and I walked all the way across it, meeting
nobody. It was my best day, the one
I always use in my letters home and look for,
year after year, when I go back or see
New York in a movie. It will never turn up.

It will persist as a detail remembered
out of context, daring me to fit
it into some good story I can't imagine.
Always, the same adamantine buildings
rise up out of the bare trees as I
make nothing out of them except a romance

in which I do not appear. And so even the best day
is a light to fail by, and my joy
a lucent hazard I cannot avoid
too long. Too often, it is as if that hazard
moved, staying one step ahead of me. This morning,
I walked back into the field behind my house

and one patch of sky was a blue screen receding
across the bare ground, leaving a wild design
of settled birds and thin ice in the furrows.
There was no place for me anywhere in that field.
But as I stood there, an unnecessary
glad witness, I kept trying to think of one.

A Setting

in memory of John Cheever

There is nothing Orphic, nothing foreign.
The deep greens of a suburban June,
the lawns, the orientalia,
are enough, for now, to make you sing.

The deep greens of a suburban June
drift from oriel to oriel and
are enough, for now, to make you sing
into the dark you've watched

drift from oriel to oriel. And
now the air around the porchlights curves
into the dark you've watched,
changing into the colored air of romance.

Now the air around the porchlights curves
like hours in summer, like desire,
changing into the colored air of romance
your first home breathed into you.

Like hours in summer, like desire,
what you cried out each June
your first home breathed into you,
became the best of you.

What you cried out each June—
"There is nothing Orphic, nothing foreign!"—
became the best of you,
the lawns, the orientalia.

The Gaza of Winter

The frail smoke and virtues of the season blind
us, almost with hands, and which of us can instruct
the other now? I will have to find your body
shifting at the edge of your last word.
You will have to find whatever I could mean
by groping along that same edge. And all of winter
will be ground to nothing in a slow mill

of smoke and virtue. We are bound to that mill,
and our cold seeking and shifting is the blind
set task of that bondage, cruellest in winter.
What does it matter that we love and instruct
our hearts rightly? I have lost the way to your body.
You have lost the way to know what I mean
when I curl up inside every word

you speak as if it were your hand. A word
is as close as I can ever come. This winter,
we have been forced to understand the blind
distance between virtue and a body
bound up in nothing it could ever mean.
A marriage is Gaza. Ours is blind at a mill
now, every turn of which seems meant to instruct

the dark in darkening, hearts in how to instruct
themselves in spite. There will be blanks instead of words
from now on, a grist of silence for the mill.
But why is it I still think of going blind
with you as my life's work? In our first winter,
I followed you up the steps to where your body
slipped out of gray ice and lit the mean

rooms wonderfully. What would happen if those mean
rooms turned up again, a few steps from the mill
we turn? Would anything about them instruct
us in how to live there as we did, all winter,
curled up in the smoke and virtue of blind
first nights and first days? I wish that every word
I knew were a step back to them. A body

should give off more than light if anybody
is to go on thinking of it not meaning
to go crazy. I should do more with the words
I know than make puzzles. A life's work can instruct
a life or can lead it in bondage to a mill
of bad marriage, bad silence, and a blind
refusal to accept that in one winter

everything can go right, then wrong. The winter
I followed you up your steps is over. Your body
is wrapped in its own words now and cannot mean
what I wish it did. I think of years of mill
work ahead, grinding down a store of words
you will not hear me say, living to instruct
a puzzled heart in how to live blind.

No Valediction

I want to uncurve us from the bedpost's polished
glass and cannot. We stay there, flailing just
beneath the surface of the light we darken
with dark eyes and our bodies using the light
to flail. The bedroom window is all sky.
If I could fill it with you, I'd be alone.

In the mornings, I remember less than ever.
The days lie straight out of the room and only
begin to curve hours later, turning away
from every surface polished enough to catch light
or the two of us as we still are.
If this goes on for long, I will always love you.

Consenting

In your best dream, everything responds
and smiles with the loving awkwardness,
the sudden blurred readjustments of
a group photograph. There is a word
for everyone. There is a sky
filled with the tops of trees and letters
hanging from them, spelling your name.

All the answers you can accept
begin there. Rooted, like ideal
children, in that locale where answers
are things you touch, they wear the features
of a world too easy to fail
or be struck dumb. They sing to themselves.
They cheerfully explain that gardens

flourish without you, that the tall,
bright windows that look onto gardens
shine because there is no one in them.
A comfort, an accounting for absence
signed with your own name. You can
walk out into the afternoon's
exact center and disappear,

knowing, now, that what becomes
of you has a place reserved among all
the words and smiles you have arranged
in your best dream. Which is to say
that the world loves you back and is changed
permanently by what you do.
As simple as that. To want some things to live

because they will live anyway,
to look at a photograph
of strangers waving up to you
from a garden somewhere in New Haven,
makes your share of the world possible.
It adds a name to the list. It fills
the sky with the tops of trees and letters.

Emily Dickinson's Mirror, Amherst

Its flecked surface a map of disappearing islands,
the glass imposes a narrowing, flat sense
of time and limited space upon the room
at all angles. Looking into it head on,
I feel contained and ready to understand
the short lines' skewed New England syntax mouthed
into so strict a frame. A discipline
of words arrayed for the bridal and no groom
wanted. In each of us, there must be one
oracular, strait emptiness a hand's
breadth across that is ourselves in proud
fear, looking into our own eyes for doctrine
and the one audience whose accents we can
wholly share. The purist's God. Pride's mirror and island.

FROM

New Dark Ages

Survey

I am so lonely for the twentieth century,
for the deeply felt, obscene graffiti
of armed men and the beautiful bridges
that make them so small and carry them
into the hearts of cities written like words
across nothing, the dense void
history became in my beautiful century.
When a man talks reason, he postpones something.
He gets in the way of a machine that knows him
for the sad vengeance he is, somewhere close
to the bald name of his city. "New York"
means "strike back." "Attica" means "strike back"
and so does anyplace in the world
in the huge eyes and tender hands of my century.

I went to the capital. I had a banner,
and there were thousands of people like me.
There was an airplane, and for a moment
heavy with laurel and sprays of peach blossom
something that had never happened before
stretched like a woman's shadow on a hedge
between the plane and the people who saw it flying.
It was the real name of the century.
It told everyone to strike back
until there was no reason in the world
except a machine stalled overhead
that knows everyone and is as delicate
as peach blossom. But the poor years come too late.

1848

Uneven sounds whiten the pavements
after nightfall. The tall hats of rebellion
have taken on a life of their own,
floating and rearranging tirelessly
over the pavements of the old streets
which by 3 AM are white as bones.

Every hour of my sleep is a useless rebellion.
I dream that you return to hear one last
argument, to touch my face in the hallway
a last time before the interdiction,
the yellow bulb between apartments
sputtering like a bad kiss as you go.

Justice demands that no one be loved for himself.
Freedom demands that each kiss be a contract
between desire and the unformed constellations
of all objects—whatever is dreamed,
whatever is stolen from the thief of possession,
whatever strikes the bone of pavement

as a woman steps out of a tenement
into the permanent rebellion
of which she is blameless. In 1848
the social contract becomes a horrid loneliness.
Justice abandons freedom, and freedom
begins to think of itself as a new star,

a light in a hallway and then a thousand lights
careering over the bones of uneven pavement.
When I lie down in bed tonight
I will think of a new argument
to turn the tide of rebellion against freedom,
to press hands to faces until they touch bone.

How Passion Comes to Matter

When I was a boy, my father drove us once
very fast along a road deep in a woodland.
The leaves on the trees turned into mirrors
signaling with bright lights frantically.
They said it was the end of the world and to go faster.

I am beginning to know in whose name
the uprisings, the sudden appearances
of facades like damp cloths, somehow happen.
Think, for me, of a woman thrown
in front of a train. You can see her

falling in the staccato of her last gesture,
that little wave, and she will never stop
leaving you, just as you will never find
a kiss that can move faster than a train.
Or think, rather, of a boy

who felt the death inside his first lover
and went home and died of gunshot in his sleep.
I know there is a cult of such things—the young dead.
I understand the excess they cause.
But as passion is their signature, admit

we are grief-sodden and thus romantic.
We raise no columns in the great style but only
the anxious facades of left-wing cities
never to be completed. She brings
a damaged son and an open mouthful of milk

to one who is always leaving her, and she
reappears suddenly under the low and inwrought
housefronts of April, that month teeming
with slaughter. It is the pause of the world.
Time triumphs in an incompleteness we can feel

on each other's bedding. In the unstill noise
of couples, high, shameless operas prove
the truth of uprisings, guiltless trains, gunshots
in a boy's sleep. Father drove us very fast.
In left-wing cities, we can drive no faster.

The Northeast Corridor

The bar in the commuter station steams
like a ruin, its fourth wall open
to the crowd and the fluttering timetables.
In the farthest corner, a television
crackles a torch song and a beaded gown.
She is my favorite singer, dead when I was born.
And I have been waiting for hours for a train,
exhausted between connections to small cities,
awake only in my eyes finding shelter
in the fluttering ribbon of shadow
around the dead woman singing on the screen.
Exhaustion is a last line of defense
where time either stops dead or kills you.
It teaches you to see what your eyes see
without questions, without the politics
of living in one city, dying in another.

How badly I would like to sleep now
in the shadows beside real things or beside
things that were real once, like the beaded gown
on the television, like the debut
of a song in New York in black and white
when my parents were there. I feel sometimes
my life was used up before I was born.
My eyes sear backwards into my head
to the makeshift of what I have already seen
or heard described or dreamed about, too weary
not to envy the world its useless outlines.
Books of photographs of New York in the forties.
The dark rhombus of a window of a train
rushing past my train. The dark halo
around the body of a woman I love
from something much farther than a distance.

The world is insatiable. It takes your legs off,
it takes your arms and parades in front of you
such wonderful things, such pictures of warm houses
trellised along the sides with green so deep
it is like black air, only transparent,
of women singing, of trains of lithium
on the awakening body of a landscape
or across the backdrop of an old city
steaming and high-shouldered as the nineteen-forties.
The world exhausts everything except my eyes
because it is a long walk to the world
begun before I was born. In the far corner
the dead woman bows off stage. The television
crumples into a white dot as the last
train of the evening, my train, is announced.
I lived in one place. I want to die in another.

The New World

A little emptiness beforehand,
and then I take up the exhausted
slogans, the party of one whose single issue
is a house a little above street level,
the remote handiwork of the ironmonger
like a signature afloat in porchlight,
a place you do not have to carry with you
as I carry mine out of a little emptiness
into bad museums where I spend time.

Every man's routine is fantastic.
Read the transcripts. Spend some time
bent over the glass cases reading spider diaries
and opaque, absolutely usual daybooks
of the colonists. Obsessed with the familiar
(as we are not), with death in a spinney
or underneath an uncleared half-acre,
they recount nothing. And even nothing is so private
the handwriting crooks into scythes and obscenities.

In the next room, a handful of religious paintings.
A little emptiness in the faces,
especially in the eyes of the Christ child
staring away from His Mother.
Often, she was the painter's mistress posed
as Mary. She looks frightened, perhaps of blaspheming
or of being beaten by the rogue who paints her.
I stand as close to the pictures as I can.
The cracks in the paint flourish like handwriting

or like new streets from the air,
so much personal history dispersing
leaving only the false record of sentiment,
the old religion of the Puritan daybooks.
Life leaves nothing behind itself. Culture
is the traduction of routine
under the yellow light of museums, an emptiness
old and new, level with the street.
Outside, the remote handiwork of traffic makes no sound.

The Night Orchard

They have given me a room near the power station
across the canal, and sleeplessness has become
an island jolted by hot sounds and water lights.
A vapory static scents the air like fruit
that has caught fire. Thickly, the shallows
of a dream that I would have if I slept
darken under a greasy skin that won't break.
And then the scent of fire again, sweet, heaviest
near a woman's letter to me, propped on the nightstand.

As you near the center of America,
you reach an unmoving inland sea of towns
founded, strange to say, on a migration
fleeing tolerance. The coastal cities
had accommodated small boroughs of affection.
Their harbors steamed with tenderness at morning,
and at day's end a borderless sublime
floated in the bankers' streets and you
might put it in your soft hand and then

into a friend's hand like clean money.
And so the undistracted governments
of heaven fled inland, upwelling
and lacustrine charters of orchards, tulip farms,
and, in the next century, power stations
and bad hotels to afflict the transient.
Borne up and eddied in sleeplessness there,
in nearly a fever dream, I can sense orchards
burning and power becoming water again.

Absurd, because this isn't Florida.
They do not drive off frost with fires
in orchards as they do in orange groves.
Power stations do not spew forth shipwreck;
they light houses; they hang dry and solid
in their constant translating stammer.
But I am afloat somehow, and there is the sweet of burn.
What, if anything, upholds a person
cut off from the mercy of his private life

remembering the little flecks of burn
on skin where there had been no fire
but his mouth only and at morning patches
of white like sea mist? What is there to translate
at the center of America but roiling
shallows and, away inside you,
an answer to the letter on the nightstand?
The questions that we ask of the civil world
leave us one choice: either freedom

is identical with happiness or we are all
on islands in the middle of flat continents
jolted by the stammer of sleepless dreaming.
The money of countries must feel like a skin
or it is rubbish. I must be able to stand
in the center of the night orchard
and be touched by fires burning justly
in the good tolerance of the landowners.
I must answer a simple letter

with language wrought from my heart's error,
common to everyone by example, but belonging
solely to one woman whose body is sea mist
and whose voice over the telephone sounds so
much like wings that it must be wings
grown out of the flecks of burn along her shoulders
sometime after I left her bed
and she began to write such beautiful letters
addressed to hotels. Finally, the power of inland

cities must be a charter of the heaven
curled on apple leaves, small and perfectly
suspended between happiness and freedom
on one stem. As we come closer to a real sleep,
as we get that far, America is purely
and completely its center, down to the seas
in all directions. Its sweet produce
always afire, in winter and in summer.
The question of our civil lives stammers

between legislating the difference
and knowing the difference that sets
each heart away on islands, and it tries to speak
out of itself of the loving error of passion
which is the beginning of freedom
which is the beginning of happiness.
I have my answer. She has always known it.
I bury it and my face in her shirt. Great turbines
and little coins like new Floridas spin in the dark.

The Judas Nocturne

Twilight is espionage conducted openly,
groups of unhappy men in topcoats peering
into ground-floor windows. How lovely
if the fate of nations flowered and collapsed
into little rooms at street level, rooms like mine
where I am just explaining to someone
that she is a cloud chamber of furtive stars
and that I have a map of them.

Modern times are an awkward spectacle.
On the one hand, our public selves compete
for scarce window space, for the opportunity
to see in to where power is decided
and used. On the other, private life
recedes like a glacier, a translucent corner
of heaven meant only to be photographed,
never settled. And each detests the other

even inside us. I try to tell a woman
I love her and can't go to bed with her,
afraid as I am of the least darkness:
my shadow floating over her stomach; the deep
pencil lines in her hair and in her eyes.
Her small chin falling to her breast
the way a spark falls in a cloud chamber
tells me that I am a liar and a bad man,

just as huddled topcoats at the window
and fretful looks the mirror-image of mine
tell me I am the class enemy
of decent feeling, of the family troikas
clustered on islands of public recreation
in calm sunlight. I should go to bed with the woman.
I should find a hillock in the dark
and sleep until the morning when there is work

and nothing to be afraid of. How
can I explain that fear is the last, abused rite of freedom?
I fear losing her, so I must lose her.
I am afraid one morning I will have no window space
and no access to power, so I tell lies and steal things.
She has little breasts and wears a perfume
named for groves in Syria. My rooms
are almost heaven. When I was in school

I made a cloud chamber for my science class.
Inside it, the seeds of cosmos
sprouted in bad air, burned, and disappeared.
I never saw anything so pretty
until I saw the words *adultery* and *treason*
printed large in a manuscript about hell.
It was a clumsy bit of medievalism
but larger than the world, brighter than the end of the world.

Wartime

All the more beautiful in the concert hall
with people in their fine clothes and yourself
in the same place as the original music.
The rest, I imagine, must be like the sound
of a radio orchestra in the nineteen-forties,
Europe fiddling beneath the darkness,
and those abandoned in the capital cities
leaning into the sound as it becomes noise.

Our lives seldom advance. And the beautiful
is a principle either too large
or too small to contain so much loose
and indispensable striving.
That is why I think of music, why I love
even the idea of an orchestra
in the open spaces of the outdoors
and worried corners of rooms during the blitz, my love's last hours.

They do not move much, but they are real.
They live in the anticipation
and in the backwards aftermath. They feel
light canceling the illumination
of the previous moment when I told you
Europe was dead. Mahler already knew.
That is why I said that being inside of you
is the harsh Symphony and withdrawing from you

a song at the end, something of the earth
too large for desire, too small to survive.
And these analogies are still nowhere
close to you, close to me, who are trying
so hard to believe that things
are not the hallucinations of bad history
or of autumn settling into its long self-pity
of mists and overripeness apt not to change.

In early November, the city parks hum
beneath the thinnest frost. The couples
and solitaries have got it wrong at the
lake's edge, feeding the birds, saying
nothing to themselves or to each other
about the coming holidays, the anticipation
buried close by, in the wrong place perhaps,
but someplace. It fills the earth like music.

Least Said

One little turbulence, a candle lit
in the hollow of a wall near the site
of executions. It was far too late
in the clumsy, ordinary hour of his defeat
for the invader to destroy them in any
order. Too late for terror. Time only
for the haphazard, panicked assembly
in the marketplace, and then the peppery
sounds and the bodies like incomplete signatures.

The autonomy of the dead is of no use
and has no memorial. It insists
that life is better purposeless
than committed to the bad devices
of perfection, better unremembered
than lionized among all the faceless lions
crouched along the remote spandrels
of official grief. The dead
accept no communion and rally to no sound.

That is their freedom. The fences and chiming poplars,
and then nothing. The buoyancy of redheads
in soft dresses, and then nothing. A hurried
sentence constellated in the pearly
accents of one rushing up a staircase,
and then nothing. Our freedom is that sharp line
drawn by the dead between a thought
untranslatable, asocial and the use of death
by thoughtless contrivers of memorials

whose purpose is beyond freedom and of no help.
We batten our days within strict limits.
Our small apartments contain less than we imagine,
and imagination is a frayed thing stretched too far.
Occasional, generous lovers shimmer briefly

and in the small hours take to the stairs.
We do not call after them, or we call
too softly to be heard. Their sudden absence
is Paradise and needs no memorial.

Production Number

All are frantic, like water flowers.
Dancing in the sharpest outlines they can manage,
the poorly loved, the compulsive
cartoon posters of women dancing at all angles
on the hoardings of cities in slant rain—
so many flowers in a tempest,
so many arms or fine legs broken to shards.

It must be popular, this crazy angling
for self-knowledge in the suffering of others,
especially of women. In the music of the 1920s
it turned the bridges of New York into arrows.
In the posters of Weimar it turned dancing
and beautiful women in repose
into bad engines, windmills of swords.

Ours is the century of popular death.
Our music keens at the tall centers of bridges.
Our poetry mimics the fast poison of dancing
because it loves women best when they dance
too quickly, their bodies the beautiful weapons
of the posters, of the bridges of New York,
of what it could love, groaning in Weimar.

We belong to death. It makes us famous.
Gershwin wanted to write serious music, and he did,
and the 1920s learned to use the bodies of dancers
as brass and drum and as a stamping chorus of engines
on the weightless, insupportable bridge of the next decade.
There was no next after that, and I can only
imagine what might have been, the same as you.

The Old Causes

"My soul is wearied because of murderers."—Jeremiah 4:31

In the cool future, one will put off her dress by a window
and another will make the choice
between inhabiting and admiring.

We don't live long enough, any of us, to outlast history.
We shall not love with our bodies again
except in the coronal streets of paintings,

the unjust happiness and lamplight of the ratty voyeur
for ones so terribly thin now
without the little flags of their clothes.

Great tyrants understood the flesh and our nostalgia for it.
The glory of the rainy square
alive with atoms of loud speech . . .
The glory of oblique pillars
of sunlight on the tousled hairs of a bed . . .
The glory of not taking you in my arms now
but letting the paradise of the next day
waken to find you already there
teaching me to live with no purpose
and the endless rain on the public square better than heaven.

I dream of the deprived utopias that may yet arrive.
I see myself repeating a kind of courtship.
There is a messy apartment
brightened here and there by the subjective icons
of a woman's life before I knew her.
Somehow, I translate all of that
into the struggle and final triumph
of all of the people shouting one name,
not my name, but one I know intimately,
and then it is my right to go to bed with her.

In the cool future, the apartments and unfeeling icons
will face each other across our bodies.
We shall count for very little

or maybe I shall have learned to make the right choice, tendering
the little flags of her clothes
between my hands like a birthplace

or like the silhouette of my mother by the broken glass
of the apartment she died in
crowned with the future's coronal of lamplight.

Against Pluralism

Whom will you point to? In the needle's eye,
or selling what you own at the strait gate,
who will know how to kiss you and just when
to pull the hair at your neck and say your name?
No single victim will ever be the last.
Not, at least, until one victim purifies
the whole issue of suffering
by crying out that his pain means nothing
because it comes from nowhere and goes nowhere.
The clusters of exiles in their storefronts
will be free then. History will end.
Lover will take her hand from her lover's mouth
and see only his mouth, not a sightless
fish's eye scored onto the sheet's marble.

It's a wise child who knows he is no angel.
The rest of us grow up hovering, visiting
our lives in the moment of pain or orgasm
or when the little fingers of pity push
inside us and we feel loved. Our suffering
gales beneath our wings like applause.
We long to repeat it, to explain it
to stay aloft and clear of our lives in that
mid-heaven of nostalgia and apology.
We hover over the camps, the forced retreats,
the ends of nations that no one can recall now
except as code words for catastrophe.
We alight for pleasure, touching the victims
as the hurt husband touches the bed his wife has left.

Father loved you with a passion. Or else
from fear of your long, inarticulate future,
he turned silent, edging into crank broadcasts
by a small radio on the screened porch.
Perhaps, as my father did, he moved out
into another house and had a daughter
with a redheaded woman who mistook his silence

for grief. My father never lost anything.
For years, I went to school with the daughter
as she grew fat and her red hair reached her knees.
Who were the victims? At what moment
should my father have cried out, the mothers
have cried out, or I have taken the fat hand
of my sister and walked off through the needle's eye?

And it's a wise child who can understand
that the mothers and fathers on the trains
see only the receding pastorals,
the lamplit villages of other angels,
and that his suffering is only one pinpoint
on a lithic hoarding of departures
each passenger reads like an advertisement of heaven.
The wise child goes crazy. How could he not?
How could he not be heartbroken to learn
that even compassion is compassionless, that it uses
the real or imagined pain of others and himself
for wings, for memory, for a marriage proposal,
for the cruel angelism that adores victims
and makes a fifth, airier element out of pain?

We recede. We recede. A virus finds
that place deepest behind the heart where it
unweaves itself into a pattern of false starts
like knots of villages and the one house
lightening at the crest of a green street
as its doors close to us. Dearest,
that is another crime of pluralism.
Hope, jagged with beginnings, scatters
our one real life among a dozen houses,
little illnesses of longing whose low
fevers contract the heart. You have but one heart.
And I have one. At the crest of a green street
we give them away. The night thanks us.
The fences shiver with cats, and the flowers close.

Feeling comes from nowhere and goes nowhere.
It is not a train. It is not one instance
of lovemaking or a lifetime spent together
running the dogs, dying finally face down
in the yard bed of herbs. We are all the same.
Or, rather, we should believe we are the same
in order to be happy with the same things
and not to be stealing from each other.
We put each other in camps. I crush my lover with a kiss
and then it is impossible to love her.
What must die if we are to live without barbed wire
and bad sex is the very idea of otherness.
And to kill the idea, we have merely to find
one victim in ourselves who will die for nothing.

My father could not stop getting children.
The people on the trains cannot stop watching
the passing villages for their own ghosts
and early angels. I cannot stop finding
houses in which to lose my heart a dozen times
in the fits and starts of a little passion exalted.
Life is not going to be bearable, I think,
for a long time. The exiles will play cards
in their storefront lodges. History will slide on.
And one will pull the hair at my neck. And one
will cover my mouth as she makes love to me.
The streets are snowed in under heaven's leaflets.
Our beds are scored with sightless eyes, the eyes of others.
The air is sickeningly heavy with applause.

New Dark Ages

The loose stonework and an outdated sense of freedom
like the word *airship* or like the fragmentary
sense memory I have of reading books in a cloister
on my birthday when the sunlight is always pure.
These things slip from the rail of a long terrace.
They fall into the street and past it, into the river.
And inside me, the airship lifts and swells
and people in turn-of-the-century costume
laugh with amazement as the loose stonework
and our lives fall as the airship rises.

I've never had much real control over things.
The music of pianos, for example, is the dead world
where I loved the machine of my small freedoms,
one of the crowd in his best clothes despite the weather,
the Eastern snow like the distinct sound of pianos
over the airfield. The music lifts and swells.
I remember this or that. And then a loose stone falls,
and I am alone on the terrace of the longest,
best century, looking into the air for music
where there is none, all of it disappeared—
stonework breaking the surface of a river,
the lyric snow a thousand atoms of silence
skating over the surface. All I've ever done
is to wait, to gasp at the take-off and flight
of what I just barely feel. My freedom
as it was taken away early.
The sunlight stilling a cloister on my birthday.

The air is filled with ships.
A machine plays many pianos at once,
and the music holds them aloft, a different tune
for each ship. Freedom has nothing to do with control
and control nothing to do with my weak heart
lonely for its birthday and the excitement
of pure sunlight and of snow parting

into countless buoyant shapes over the airfield.
A long, long century is crumbling around me.
There is much to remember, and I want
to give it all away, to become lighter than air.

FROM

Erasures

Muse

You are somewhere very close to the porch.
The evening makes crazy sounds, but makes sense.
The unpackaged, greeny neighborhood settles
into true night far from the expressway
and farther from the calligrams of the downtown.
The visits to the paintings failed me.
The new music faded underground with the last trains,
with stripped hours and many lovers.

I did not imagine a stronger life,
listening for your step on the porch step,
imagining your dress a size too large
billowing the obscene print of summer.
Anything composed is an obscenity:
a painter's phlox in vertical brushstrokes;
a dressmaker's parody of stupid earth;
a radio's jazz clawed by cats.

A stronger life exists but is no one's friend.
She lives in the crook of the expressway
in a high building. She tucks her hair behind
her ears and carries a clear drink to the window.
No one ever paints her portrait. Her name
is ugly and can't be put to music.
And at her neck and ankles a long dress
blackens calligrams I read with my fingers.

The truth of those black messages is cold.
The imagination has no power over life,
and between inspirations that are lovers
and inspirations that are a kind of machinery
repainted every year but irreparable
the only thing actual at day's end
is night's uncomposed, leafy tunelessness.
I will not open the door when you arrive.

I will not call my lost loves to wish them well.
In my house in darkness behind the porch
I pound the walls and make an animal noise
as the neighborhood rises and runs en masse
onto the expressway to be destroyed
or dragged downtown to touch the calligrams
and feel nothing that is green, made, or harmonious.
It is loveless time, the neck and ankles of time.

I need more loneliness than alone is,
the deep, uninspired dark of America
where sexy lawns, the phlox, the print dresses
and hymn stanzas like tiny, circular railroads
ask for no response and no love
but a clear drink in the solitary evening
when no muse visits, when crazy animal sounds
make sense and I read the truth with my hands.

The Lesson of the Classics

The remaining oracles were obscene,
like unfolding a towel and finding maggots there
and the next moment a detonation of green

flies. So many sexual martyrs had tied
machinery to their sallow backs, their weedy
shoulders, hoping monstrousness might revise

the brutal logarithm of excess
tenderness, of man and woman with Iphigenia
who must die, of government that must undress

the condemned in open court before they die.
The love of honor became murder.
Human, purposeful embraces at night

became machinery on a martyr's back.
If you have a family, starve them.
If your passport lies open on the desk

of a stranger, man or woman it makes no difference,
your life ended an hour ago.
There on the desk, your inverted face

in the passport photo sobs and twists
farewell as if it were already on fire.
If you have a child, you kissed it

for the last time an hour ago.
They are strapping something to its back,
the shape of an olive tree, the size of snow.

Infant spittle beads like mercury
on the temple pavement. It is an oracle,
caustic ichor of many victories.

Heat Lightning

We are living in the beautiful district.
The wind lets no leaf touch the ground.
Next door, in bright sun, a girl on stilts
is so fabulously illuminated
she blends into the light below her legs.
We are a people without holidays.

On the old street, men would kill their wives
for a stiff wind. Their freedom was laws,
and their lives stank. No one is healthy
where discarded children return cureless
and the wind's telegraphy on flagpoles
(colonial savage other) speaks
the fates of animals, the edicts of holiday.

Concede a limb to save a limb, an eye
for an eye that looks outward only.
My heart was a sieve of law and had
no reward but another child's slower illness
on the ward where they made Christmas in July
and every month. The stockings never came down.

On the old street, sacrifice depended
upon faith. In the beautiful district,
light stands firm beneath the children,
I live alone, undiscarded, and
sacrifice is the ordinary of each day.
Sun and wind intensify
without interruption and we blend
to one color the color of windows.

If she were small enough, in the complete darkness, she could sleep between the strings. Music untitles the Jew of summer, a species of angel. The stylus reaches all the way across the alley. Sleeping there, the perfect soprano wears every surface of her body to bed. The starlight also reaches her, no one to say otherwise.

Erasures

The monument is in throes.
Where such ferocity comes from
the leaf scorches,
the linen of the workers' hostel
decorates like a sunflower
in a sandpainting.

She says nothing, and it sells. The flooded stairwell undulates limb and limb, the key of a city with no sky. The distance put to music, my jalousie, tell me the night was unextinguished by the lamps. The house is to let.

Out of the heart of one string
came Pierrot the Stateless.
How he rose to power,
organized the militias around
a vial of clear liquid,
scorched the linen where he lay.
Never mind. He loved always.

It was and was. I sat in a tiny airplane and the scenery defied hallucination. Have you forgotten, composition by tones and daggers made these beautiful valleys, these clockwork villages? Ungrateful now, as every pharmaceutical is ungrateful to the illness, the good folk spit into icons only the snow loves, in little mounds, in a bird's track.

Was and was.
By unexpected heat
unrounded, the balloons
rise all the same.
Our war rises all the same,
though its deformities
cartoon the sky.
They distract our astonishment
from its true architecture:
in the stairwells, floodwater.

Apart from Solitude

In late autumn, dark birds darken against
sunrise in the catalpa till they are a stone's weight.
The dying bee attacks the swollen spider
to no profit. Late abed against the chill
of morning, couples exchange the musty consent
of their bodies out of genuine love
and travel the long slide of the late autumn
into unhappier, deeper chills
the springtime will do nothing to warm.
Their loving consent disenfranchises them.
Which is to say they have agreed to lie apart
from solitude, man's and nature's original
crisis and tenure. I went out early
to have my winter coat on and to see my breath.
In the next street from mine, there was a child
in her bare feet staring up into the trees.
She saw the birds there, huge with stillness in the cold.
She told me they were kittens and that I
should bring them down to her. I walked away.
It was too early in the day and too early
in the unpartnered time of the girl
to explain or even tell her of the morning
of my fourth birthday when I saw what she saw
and called the kittens down. They came to me,
and I began to enjoy the feeling of love,
began that early to be dead to the world,
to have no voice in its government or nature.

Last

The unsigned architecture of loneliness
is becoming taller, finding a way farther
above the horizontal flowering
of the Cold War, the peonies
and star asters of wild partisanship.
I have a shambling gait and lonely
hysteria, but no Terror. I am free
to shamble past the vacant lot of my son's
conception, to shamble past the bar where I
conceived adultery as a Terror
that would be endless, flowering
in great waves through air striated like chenille.
I walk for a long time and try to conjure
elsewhere in its early isolation.
I cannot. It is all redestinated
by the future like the loose balloons
a janitor recovers at 6 AM
from cold light fixtures. The Cold War is ending.
Buildings are taller and have no names.

I.

The romance of every ideology
torments the romance of another. How
beautifully, in the beginning, in
the gale and embrace of isolation, boys
capered over a shambles and swore oaths.
The scent of urine in the hall at home
was righteousness. The beautiful nude
obscured by dust in a paperweight
was righteousness. Neglectful townships coming
into steep flower just as boys were flowering
needed the correction of righteousness,
the horizontal slag of government
by children. Only the insane allegiances
endure. The mad counterparts are lovers

passion cannot explain nor circumstance
restrict to the dead zones of irony.
A counterpart of the end of the Cold War
is adultery. A counterpart
of loving a divided Berlin
unto death is fatherhood, the doting
maintenance of sons in vacant lots
continuing the wars of rubble
for righteousness' sake and for the sake
of nudes obscured by dust and vulgarity.

Romance torments romance. The most beautiful
moment of the twentieth century
galed and embraced the acrid smoky air
as the Red Army entered Berlin,
as Hitler shriveled in the gasoline fire,
as Red Army flags opened above Berlin
safeguarding the ruins of a changeless future.
Townships blackened even as they flowered.
Loose balloons cluttered the low sky and sun.
I walked for a long time and tried to conjure
the form of kindness. It was a domestic
animal confused in the tall grass.
Boys set fire to the grass. History
that opens flags opened the fire,
and Berlin, divided from Berlin,
began to love its children past all reason.

2.

My son reads sermons of pain and writes on walls.
He starves the ground
he walks on, preparing a dead city
to be worthy of its new flags, to shine
as exploded windows shine, raining down
for hours after the wrecking crews have gone.
I have a lover now who hates children.
The hatred floats inside of her, a weightless
sexual pavilion of perfect form

and perfect emptiness. I thought
by making love to her I would conceive
nothing but Terror, outrage upon outrage,
a violence that would last my whole life
and free my son. I was ignorant as a balloon.

Across the luminous expressway, I see
the shapes of charred tenements castellated,
fading into the more tender shapes of night.
It may be the last night in history. Tomorrow
pulls down the Berlin Wall, pulls down my honor,
and I return to my lover's bed to float
in a white condom, no longer my son's father.
Tomorrow describes everything in detail.
It explains nothing. It does not teach my boy
that tenements are better than the future,
better than peace, more likely to produce
brothers than are the glassy hands of mornings
without end or walls denuded of their wire.
In the dead zone of irony before dawn,
only the cats cry, like martyrs in the flame.

3.

Gates everywhere. The Brandenburg. The Great
Gate of Kiev beneath which children stride
onto an invisible crescendo
disappearing into gasoline fires,
emerging as the new shapes of righteousness
in slow vans through the Brandenburg Gate.
Oaths are secret because none suspects
that they are kept. They thrust themselves towards us
unashamedly, like the insane homeless,
and we do not see them. In our loneliness,
we see a chance for love in betrayal,
not death. In our loneliness, we see the happy
triumph of glassy hands in free elections,
not the denuding of Berlin or wanderings
of children in vans reduced by fire

to black transparencies in the morning shade.
When Joan of Arc surrendered to the flames
she cried out "Jesus, Jesus." Some years later,
a failed magician who had loved her cried out
"Joan, Joan" as the flames mocked him with a sortilege
too easy to be unreal or profitable.

I walk for a long time and try to conjure
the form of loneliness without Cold War.
It is ash upon ash, a chiaroscuro
aloft and on the ground, completely still.
Oaths are secret because none suspects
the desperation of every object, the child
in every atom of the misused world
thrust towards us, crying out whatever
sacred name it witnessed put to death
on the ascending music of a wall.
Our buildings are tall and have no names.
The parks grow glassy hands instead of flowers.

4.

Afterwards, the calm is piteous
but insubstantial as a smell of burn
that does not rise in smoke or die with the fire.
Imagine walking out of a house at sunrise
and having to invent air, invent light
from nothing but untriggered memory.
All things beloved are recalled to pain.
Air recollected from the wrists of girls
braceleted for Confirmation, crossed.
Light recollected from between the cars
of night trains in a deep river valley
where islands in the river glowed like swans.
Air recollected from a ditch in flower.
Light recollected from the sex of flowers
in bare rooms, the grainy light of blondes.
Air recollected from religion.
Light recollected from the incensed clutch

of bodies before sunrise in the oaths
of a great and ignorant lost cause.

Imagine walking out of a house at sunrise
having spent the night in bed with a stranger.
Aloft and on the ground the calm
unfurls like flags without device or slogan.
The inconsequence of the day ahead
stirs airless atmospheres in darkness
visible as daylight but without shade.
Without Cold War, without the arbitrary
demarcation of cause from cause, of light
and air from the unsexed improvisations
of memory, I cannot see to walk
or breathe to breathe. Sex becomes applause.
Sex becomes television, and the bastard
avant garde of lonely architecture
breaks ground at the unwired heart of a city
that marks the capital of nothing now.

5.

A scratchy, recorded call to prayer crosses
the alley from one new building into mine.
The consolations of history are furtive,
then fugitive, then forgotten like a bar
of music that might have been obscene or sacred
once, in another city, in the days
before today. My son is well. He works
the public ground and needs no Antigone.
My lover sits beside him at dinner,
sharing a joke, unmapping the tall future
and its unbiased children, reinventing
the sexual pavilion to accommodate
plague wards. Romance forgives romance.

The early isolation of this gorgeous
century disappears into good works.
The future is best. To put a final stop

to the grotesque unmercy of martyrdom
and to the ruinous armies of mad boys
whose government is rape, whose justice
is a wall, revoke all partisanship,
adjourn the Terror. The future is best.
It unobscures the dusty nudes. It protects
the river islands and their glowing swans.
But when I need to die, who will light the fire?
What names shall I cry out and what music
burn to a black transparency in my heart?
The unborn have been revoked. They will not be kind.

FROM

Beautiful Shirt

Lyre

Before anything could happen,
flecks of real gold
on her mouth, her eyes more
convex than any others,
the ground spoke, the barrier
of lilacs spoke. What sang
in the black tree was entirely gold.
Her chair was empty.

New absence is a great fugue
dark as the underskin of fruit.
At the center of the earth
it surrounds and amplifies the dead
whose music never slows down.

She came by car. I came by train.
We embraced. It was
at the foot of a hill steeply
crowned with apples
and a ruined fortress.
Imagination did not make the world.

Sweetness is the entire portion.
Before anything could happen,
happiness, the necessary
precondition of the world,
spoke and flowered over the hill.

When I was in Hell
on the ruined palisade,
either mystery or loneliness
kissed my open eyes.
It felt hugely convex, seeing
and immediately forgetting.

By contrast, what I imagined
later was nothing.

Privacy

In the Beloved's eye or less reliable
windowframe, see the exaggerated welcome,
a willingness to become much smaller if only
in a boy's hands, to be pushed forward
by little hands into the ceremony
and cruel fanfare of a boy's attention.

This is the world as I have known it.
It has a soft outline and is easily
victimized. It allows too much. It shrinks
under even neutral scrutiny
and, having once been seen, becomes a toy.
I live alone, am thus a child. I can tell you.

We enter the tiny village with surprise,
having passed through a window or stared too long
into loving eyes to credit
such unbuilding and pressure, like coming
to the real ocean we barely remember
to see it broken by red, abrupt divers

surfacing. The silent commercial district,
the toy trees in pencil ranks, greener
as they reach the residential grid
and its fewer lights, where am I to stand
without betraying it all, without
destroying the illusion that makes it lovely?

2.

Only begin the stories, deny
the dense forward of political cities
where Heaven is a private life
among big people. Begin innocently.

I made the table large as I could
for the rebuilding of many fates.
I put it near the window
to retell the invention of small worlds
according to a music of no tone.

On the enormous table:
sheet music of summoning adagios.
On the enormous table:
the perfervid love of innocence.
On the enormous table:
the light tools of an occult exchange,
father and lover, boyhood and beloved,
when it is easy to play God.
Hell is a public life among small people.
There is a right kind of innocence,
a communication of the bodiless
at the foil edge of homemade lakes,
in the pencil shadow of tiny trees,
in the violet luster of amnesia,
private in the midst of giants,
pointing to Heaven as toys point to a condom.

3.

Only begin the stories, shared with many.
In the harmless espionage of today,
emptiness is zeal. Only look away
to the unpunctuated trainyards between
Heaven and Hell, where childhood survives,
where leaves cup water, where time is pendant.
When I look at anything for a long time,
it shrinks down to a toy. An eclipse,
my own shadow, darkens the tabletop.
In that timeless evening: illuminations;
residences; railway lines reaching out
to cities they have no intention of reaching.
Spring arrives in trees it will not abandon,
not ever, and when the light returns

it chevrons the streets with pencil lines.
Emptiness is zeal, and unbelief
ventriloquizes liberal nature.
And before that? I heard the opening
measures of a new adagio.
They made me feel that my life was horrible
with self-knowledge, sheer size, loneliness.
I kept that music a secret,
hearing it only in the abandoned
middle places between home and work,
unending disclosure and revision.
When I listened, time pinned itself down
like green felt at the corners of a table
which is a placid field worthy of the dream
of perfect community, America without travel,
love without interrogation
in the harmless, tiny wattage of the lamps.
Everyone lives forever if he keeps his secrets.
The unbuilding and pressure of repetition
relent as time lies down with the lion
and the railway timetables yellow
in the toy station from which none departs
as none arrives. They have all disappeared
into the middle places. They have all
sheltered in the tents of their own shadows,
listening to music that promises
privacy without end and many faces,
nothing to know, no size, much company.

4.

Time to forget all lions but the mild lion
of the Peaceable Kingdom in the sudden
change and consent of a sequestered valley
where a son is born and liberal
questions as to love's brevity, passion's
eclipse, dissolve into quiet rehearsal
of the easy hymns of a minor paradise,
no longer afraid of Heaven's secrecy,

Hell's secrecy and disenfranchisement.
There comes a day when you cannot revise
your life. It is a beautiful day.
There comes a day when the urge to remain
mysterious dies into the communication
of tenderness, a guarded township
of mortalities. It is a good day.
Forget the lions. Abstractions
that are still true, though weightless,
have cleared a table in front of a window,
and the construction begins.

You could do it tonight if you wanted.
If you could become small and bless
the eclipse that is your certain death,
the adagio re-echoing forever
inside a covered bridge in New England
over the consonants of a minor river,
Housatonic or Connecticut,
out of the autumn that will not arrive,
flowing neither upwards nor down but settled
into a skein of foil that could not drown a soul,
you could do it tonight.
Forget the killing lion as you forget
the sharp jewelry of your public life.
Remember the first prayer you were taught: to be
forgotten; to be fit for a toy's life,
not wishing to communicate anything,
not wishing past the violet amnesia
of holidays and a boy's dependency.
Forgetfulness is where life found my life,
beyond which everything is inhuman,
behind which everything is commerce.

5.

Adagios. Democracy.
The sons that I might have instead of money.
Their hands are the entire sky

over the toy town, dark as only innocence,
that perfect destroyer, is dark. The hands
place a metal figurine from the 1940s,
a figure-skater with jet black hair,
the flesh of her legs chipped and silvery,
onto the tin foil at the tree-lined
edge of town. All the lamps come on.

Why have I chosen privacy over fullness?
Why have I chosen the strait, unmutual
loving of a small man whose heart is secrecy
and whose citizenship only that of the
reformed transient in the waste places
he fills from himself alone?
These are the faces beside a sleeping lion:
innocence, the destroyer of wildness;
wildness, the victim of an idea that says
virtue is denial, betrayal
of the too-full fullness of the world;
the pretty skater featured like flawless ice.

By things deemed weak subverting worldly strong,
destroying the whole network of identities
I made by being in love sometimes
and by moving from one place to another,
from widowhood to widowhood, deprivation
to deprivation, the whole lovely
business of America that traffics
in revisions of the self and the ocean
and the great land mass crushed between them.
America makes everything possible
and then deprives you of the ambition
because of its sheer size and willingness
to accommodate so many versions of yourself
not one of them ever needs be true.
And then I stole a small boy from the sea.

By things deemed weak subverting worldly strong,
seeing the ocean for the first time and seeing
it become an obscene joke of divers surfacing.

The boy and I have made a tiny village
on the tabletop of the Hudson River School
and of my father's clumsy model railroad
from the 1940s. We have drawn the curtains.
We are listening to very loud music,
adagio after adagio
by Johannes Brahms who wrote, unwittingly,
the only music true for America,
music that refuses melody,
postpones the finale in each note until
the whole thing collapses under
the burden of its possibilities.

By things deemed weak subverting worldly strong,
I have found a metallic proof
that paradise is a small place,
never jagged, flawless in its fields
and ice, not ever jagged, never
perforated or wrinkled by desire
where springtime and the days of perfect skating
lie down together with the mild lion,
and where round gestures of innocence
need no modification for the bad business
of history that limits freedom to the point
of mania and makes love impossible.
The pretty skater will not be disturbed.
The consonants of all the water in the world
will never resound near this place except
as slow, slow music falling backwards
into the first years of the Republic
when winter and spring were the same season
and the killing lion saw the ocean unbroken.

Stilling

The last snow is baited.
Where the future shatters
it unbends.
The dry bed of entirety,
where the sun bends,
shatters.

I was not afraid to tell you:
unobscene
at the first and then
the third horizon,
a copse-mountain
opened so near to me
I weighed nothing,
and you laid the flower in my mouth.

These are not animals.
These are the partial genocides
deeply uncompensated.
Under the grass
there is nothing but water
and two wings.

Plenitude

Ignore them. They are only beautiful
and heartless—not because of the unmoving
seascape behind them, the august rays crowning
pacific, glassy water in leviathan's
heavenly backdrop, but because they mean
to tell us that our freedom is a machine.
It is not. It cannot be redesigned
nor can it carry us to a new place.
We are here, where history placed us,
history that always waited modestly
for our consent, sure of receiving it.
Those beautiful young people standing
beside the automobile in the surf
agreed to nothing. If there is such a thing
as a new place, it belongs to them,
and the water will be heaven there and life
pacific in the rosy stare of the ideal.
Ignore them. Let us love our lives. No one
ever truly fled from a suburb.
He was expelled or shamed or too easily
angered. And when he left, his heart broke.
He fell easy prey to the beautiful
and to the falsehoods of seascape and landscape
with no one moving upon them as leviathan's
obsessed challenger. Our houses are buoys
set upon restless waters by strangers
dead when we were born. But we live
inside them now, and freedom is no machine
to motor us in empty circles and to raise
a round wake behind us. Freedom is a dwelling.
Sometimes, in the small arcades of a watercolor
bought at the yard sales, brass-lighted in a corner
by a chair, you have helped yourself to a dream
that drowned whalers, kin of yours, return from sea.
A holiday mood and others, like yourself,

living nearby, hurry in from the night's damp
and talk the small talk with no thought for sleeping.
Then at morning, suddenly through the west window,
birds flare golden with flying into sunrise.
It feels like driving, sometimes, but the music
is not tinny and the light is slow,
bell-towered from east to west with the morning.
Darien. Norwalk. Quaker Hill. Mystic.
Do not ignore these. Inconstant, mawkish but
deep in the old physical sense of depth,
the voluntary hours with neighbors and ghosts
teach the beauty of commuting
from dark to light, from labor to home life:
a vigilance crowned with impatience and visited
rarely but adequately by golden changes.

2.

Appreciation is mania.
Neighbors can be too many neighbors,
and cold, upturned shoals of seaboard towns
too many churches, too many conversions.

I know the stained glass above a doorway
is the discomfited piety of change
and light destroying what it makes only
to remake it more beautifully.
Such things make one thing clear: as betrayer
speaks to innocent, liar speaks to liar.

A vigil crowned with gentians
survives as disappointed love.
Visitations of impatience
take away our hands and home life.

Treason we learn from the childless small talk
of nights whose sheltering adjustments gall us.
When I first betrayed someone
an angel fell backwards through the air's sheen.

When I next betrayed someone
the air lost its heart, which is love's density.

I was at seaside in an old town,
and sea and housefronts brightened but did not open.
I was upon the point of prayer when the light
froze, converted from churchlight to porchlight.

We betray our homes because they are valuable.
No reason not to make the fine distinctions still:
we live only half-expecting the sudden flares,
or affection, or seasons out of the sea weather,
as expectations and good friends shelter by us
from the darkness of streets we've blackened together.

Five o'clock in the morning
is not four o'clock in the morning.
I have betrayed each and might betray
all in the spotless, glassy piety of change.

3.

But how hotly change limits
happiness: the small happiness of possession
and the even smaller of self-possession.
Imagine yourself transient among these houses
and the uncontrolled reflection of hotel hours
when no one in the hallway or next room
depends on you. Already, darkness covers
the tilted Common outside your window.
You hear a school band playing carols.
As always and everywhere, there are too many
drums. An hour earlier, in twilight,
you were out walking, looking into the shops,
handling the used books and scented soaps,
humming, a little abstracted by a late lunch
and the brown New England drinks hotly perfect
at Christmas. So many minutiae, so many parts
played by drums against the unsteady, truer

lines of the horns. In angular twilight,
unfocussed and sullen clusters of teen-agers,
underdressed and loudly self-aware,
anticipating nothing of change, feeling none
of the desolate childlessness of Christmas,
jostled you, marred the picturesque of the darkening
Common, and drove you back indoors.
Those same teen-agers are perfectly
reconfigured in the night now, playing
carols or holding candles as the merchants' trees
come to light. The shoppers join in then
and lift their children up to see what you
see from a hotel window: something
perfect, an incidental miracle
taking no notice of a transient
or of his cold need to interpret convincingly
accidents in the lightsome context of personal
history or a fictive changelessness.
You could be a returning mariner
stealing a welcome properly due to those
who cannot return. You feel childless
but as though a sign is coming, perhaps
from among those children out there
trumpeting mock-starlight, or from
farther away, from the black ocean beyond
the Common. Where will you not be barren?
Where will you not prayerfully resist change
to the death or to the last drum-tap
of the disorganized religion of sorrow?
Sometimes, however lonely, a wealth beyond your reach
is enough wealth, the plenitude of the lives
of strangers is enough life, enough to prove
the world adequate to desire though still strange.

4.

And when I have enough, am I afraid
no longer? When desire flutters its last

broken wheel in the red west and day
falls into the opened arms of laughter,

is it satiety or just the beginning
of fear's moment, the early dismantling
and inland birds suddenly trapped
in coastal cry, in the gulls they are not,
or is it really annihilation wrapped
in a premonition I had almost forgotten?

Between history, that topography of roofs,
and freedom, that indirect solitude
housing neither a family nor an echo
of my birth, runs a fly-blown

cheerless corridor of air.
It is the windy premonition of nothing
to desire. It lauds the greater pleasures
of the immediate present where all things
depend on paraphrase and the betrayal
of history to fiction, of freedom to delay.

Between transience, that Christmas hostelry,
and home, where I once found time to make
fine distinctions capable of taking
words or an opened hand and seeing

the democracy in it, the warm sufficiency,
runs a mania of years like atrocities.
Those years are full. They transform tirelessly
inland creatures to sea-birds, inland towns
to seaports and to submissive widows
of coastline where strangers assume the dead's renown.

Though ever strange, though nearly adequate,
the world's, or to speak honestly, my life's
suburban intervals lose buoyancy like
birds unused to tides or to wracks of net.

5.

In sinking or in being caught in nets
we find a lonely, accidental escape,
something to do with music on the radio
of an automobile, the tinny, driving, middle
distances of houses and neighborhoods
like the buoys of strangers calling us back
to life though not to our own lives, opening
as the undertow opens on the first evening
of a full moon, as sky does on the mornings
when sunrise and moonset are one hour.
I am sure that something happens.
The world is too full not to rescue
what loses buoyancy or becomes trapped.
The fullness makes a protest, and its proposal
is labor, that needle-sharp history
that follows everyone to his remote place
and serves him there. And if we refuse rescue,
we do so because we cannot believe
that fullness and innocence inhabit the same places,
haunt the same sidestreets and rock formations
in amateur choirs, in the brass-lit, private hum
of landscapes carefully miniaturized
by our pleasure in fullness and selfless love
for the ignorance swaddled in futurity
or the miraculous. These are accidental colleagues
forever bound to one another, often in love.

I got up early and went out walking
deep into woods that betrayed nothing
of ocean except the wound it makes on air.
I came to a compound barrier of rocks
beyond which I saw nothing and above which
the air was crystals of jagged salt turning
to murk. Like an exhalation, spume appeared
and then black water edging under the spray
toward me in tendrils. There was a water rat
soaked and trembling on the barrier,
coruscated, unsure of what to fear:

the advancing tide and tendriled backwash
or me, hooded in a raincoat, standing between him
and dry land, his only future and safety.
There is no difference worth noting
between thinking of oneself as "you" or "I,"
between the impostor and the true mariner.
Better to ignore the difference and believe
that the unseen ocean is no machine
but the irrepressible origin of many freedoms,
many dwellings. I stepped back into the woods,
and the rat dashed past me into common futures
of small arcades and enough welcome.

In Company

I.

A long silk
is pulled quickly
over my upturned palms
in pitch darkness. In

the horror of not being in a hurry, kneeling before a
framed numeral or tide rip or a thought of bridges, con-
fession ends. Jokes cover it like a rash, a

marlin gasping.
Music broke the
surface of my youth.
Maimed ship or maimed

voyage? When I was younger I did not need my eyes. The
world, audible in every corner, in each filter, gasped
and, glistening with seawater, made always its pavane.

By order of questions,
the toolmaking eye grows
lame. The exigency of
the gaze grows lame,

and a leaf is mistaken for floodlights. I walk beside the
highway. Even so little greenery is enough, breezy enough
to carry the whole tune, wholeness including some mountains.

Only silence
wrestles time.
Abandoned ones
stare with authority

and eat the Janus that once surrounded them. I remember how
Elizabeth died very soon after. And then Karl. A vacant ardor,
merely precarious. Their dateless echo fades, and then it swells

in music. They
drown and vanish.
They queue up, gorged
with seawater, and vanish.

The long silk moves faster and faster, cutting a channel in my
palms. The shrill perfection of our origins breaks the surface.
The fish gasp. The groves untune. Hurry vigilance, hurry.

2.

By itself, an entire
album to itself, the
snapshot of a radio
swallows fire.

The alternative is fidelity. On Saturdays, I would be taken along
to the hat shop. Between two mirrors, each one absolutely truthful,
my mother repeated, until her total absence, a horizon of nets and

false flowers.
The wounds are
insects and then
starlings, the sugar-

side of the dead. All groves whisper to the temple's benign un-
reality. I walked with you. I wore a leather coat, and I was led
away. Through gardens. The point of contact, the dirt of one letter

swallows fire.
I call it Progress.
I aim a petal of loss
instead of wheels.

We made nothing better than memory out of so much terror. In
Italy, American bombers resurrected the buried Temple of Fortune,
sheering off the rockface on a mistaken raid. Absolutely faithful,

the decisive violences
prove it to me: what is
discovered is only
spared, not sanctified.

And so my mother stood and preened, a hundredfold with her back
turned in every direction. Her absence returned from its far country,
and into the street the percussion of nets, the cornets of false

flowers poured.
No fires at all
is Progress. I
am dirt there.

A few short years afterwards, there came a superb summer. The fine
fleet had left its harbor during the night, never to return. Gardens
surfaced out of a long sleep to combat the monsters. None was spared.

3.

The father disappears into another rite.

These aggressions:
the orgasm willfully delayed;
the tulip glass left standing in the roadway.
I always hear the scream of its location.

The father is a towering furniture,
a different nudity, a different grasp.

These aggressions:
Elizabeth and Karl;
Fire and the Temple of Fortune.
And none was spared the posthumous flower
of a mother's hat.

The father cannot multiply his absence.
He rakes leaves and begins the burn.

Summer dies where his adolescent son
gorges on smoke and vanishes.

These:
beginning to burn
erodes to the status
of metaphor; the act of
forgetting indistinguishable
from remembrance except for the
body-count; mother the charnel house;
father the smoke that rises from its chimney.

Memory does not prove that something has been spared.
If I could walk or if I could breathe underwater, then
faithfulness would hurry to its aftermath, overtaking
Father above his pyre in winter sunlight, gasping.

If I could walk or if I could breathe underwater, then
summer dies where the adolescent son,
the tulip glass left standing in the roadway,
begins to burn.

A leaf is the shape of God
torn apart.
A father has no face after.

4.

Three only a little born, and then unborn. Subtract the rain
from injury and it is Saint, and it is a through-passenger.
Dunes, dunces wear the names Elaborate, Film, Basket, from
which hangs the alchemy of judicial murder. Brothers, it is im-
possible to pray to my own names. Unraveling petitions, God
is scourges, a circle of fires around the new observatory
making the stars impossible.

Three only a little born, then unborn, he pronounces tender.
First came the breast of salt, and then the breast of pine.

Earthquakes moved inland. I notice black ants erupt from the
ground to cover the walls moments before catastrophe.

If I exist, it is because my older brothers died in infancy.
I bear their names, unburdened of my own.

I get a feeling of stabbing, here, over the convulsed road.
Consolation turns mirrors to the wall, obscures angels with
snapshots. By the fireplace, on a sofa in the hotel lobby,
I drank cold wines. Across the avenue, soundless in an apart-
ment window, two naked boys slammed and slammed against
one another. They were in the custody of angels, teeth bared
from now on.

I have an ugly girlfriend. The bus fills. There are many con-
fessions, each a yellow circle of light until the foot of the
mountains, where Fortune ends. The dead are parents forgiven
by the unborn. Will you still delay?

5.

Marsh birds change direction like a pack
of cards. There is no landscape except youth,
neither end nor voice, a summer not
a venom. Father took me to a field.
Trees grew out of the stone's step-book.
And when my father struck, it was an eagle
I could not see behind my neck
but smelled its blood in my close hair.

One Sarah to John Wesley: "I know no sinners
but one, and the Devil is the other."

Too numerous too brief concord disfigured
the coat of river where I went down
to the river, disfigured the circumstances
of age in an old coat until he called
out to circumstances, to one Sarah.

The long silk neither ends nor is abolished.
Memory obeys a treble. Perfect
obedience allows me to forget
at last and to begin a real life,
music crowned by one dust and one accident.
No landscape except youth, no synagogue
except as webs shaken, and cathedrals
unborn after my brothers died monsters.

This morning, a pamphlet of cypresses
lay open on the table, covered with numbers.
I fell in love with two sides of a house,
happy for the wind's share, happy
to see the vigilance of a straight line
uproot the cypresses and drown the numbers.
It made a beautiful window in each side.

Curb

Starlings from below ground
raise street level to the level
of sustained conflict, as when
your finger disappears into the piano key
and the note, winged, sustains
to a high place.

I throw bad dice.
You genocided my wish
and my *affect*.
You were the sex
of my left eye during sex.

I cannot account for that man dressed as a friar. The time
is, at last, utterly ignorant, palsied, marching the sub-
division on a fine day. The birds bathe. A blue glove under
the snow melts to the surface.

Have it all back:
the sumptuary revolution;
the vatic streak or,
in the darkness, not
headdresses but crowns.
Have it all back.
In my left eye I saw
what befalls at the hands of children.

Thirty-nine minutes past the hour
in the white desk on the rubbish heap
balances a flirtation
and a debauchery.
Happiness has no father
nor idealist starling
to throw the good dice after bad.

Debt

Painted to the end of each
hair, in the dream-life,
the boychild seeks not me.
When the Age lays hands upon itself,
he is the hands.

Like mist close to the floor,
angels of aftermath
haunt the slaughterhouse
of this body out of mine.
The play must never start
because the stage is too beautiful.
From the beginning,

sanctity yielded
to law that yielded
to history that yielded
to aphasia. Meridian of bitter cold and strings, it never vanishes.
Beloved, approachable zero never vanishes. What it forgets or loses
enters the music by a back door, the stage so beautifully prepared.
Prokofiev dead on the same day. What must only be alone must listen.
The wilderness

dividing men from creation
wants nothing in particular
except to carry on the system
of crude barter, mouth to mouth,
without aftermath.

In a brown photograph, blind musicians carry their guitars at
chest-height. Behind them, on a public wall, the furtive, lovely
slogans of the Comintern curl into the brickwork. Innocence is
never lost. It comes constantly an infant to each wall, to every
untuned string and eye.

Utopian
vanishing
point:

The cold house grew much colder. Journalism governs everywhere
the dream-life now and blunts the profile of waking. I who was
indistinguishable
vanishing
wingspan:

Boys dancing on the Arctic Circle open the circle, driving it fast
toward us. I said nothing of my own, painted it yellow to the end.

Arranged to Meet in Aix

The career of the lakewater
entered a phase entirely
hysterical, a frenzy to be
lifelike.

By the lakeshore, a child throws a ball. The other, ignorant of
the game, retrieves it, pockets it, walks far away. A new music
advances quickly on the child, and the surface of the lake applauds.

The day arrived
as a hostage photo-
graphed holding the
newspaper announcing
his abduction. This
is a pornography
fissured by thieves.

Far out on the lake, my breast sparkles, an exaggeration of what
the photograph believes. The water is a beautiful garment suddenly
transformed into worms and serpents. Something undresses in the
woodwinds, or a man disfigures a child, over and over in the near
woodland, unheard by those dressed so brightly on the shore.

What began as a man
dying in the outside
to paint the outside
became photography
and then a music to
attenuate the skin
at the heart's surface.

A silence arouses the water and the little piles of stones. For one
moment, voracious knowledge passes from child to child like a ball.

An Instrument Also

The climate thinks with its knees.
When the wound opens, music suspires.
Opening the gate, I gain the color
below the roof tiles and the tree limbs.

You gave me
the late quartets
a black bird and
a white and the
Garden of Eden.
Your death belongs
to anyone but me.

I wonder so as not to forget. At night in Brooklyn, the tendrils
of a white sex denuded the sky, shimmering at the tall needle-
ends of buildings. The traffic was identical in the spring.

I am protected by only
music I cannot remember.
Why is it that the best
minds ended by composing
fairy tales? Death swarms.
There are many new beings,
the odor of hearts. The order

of the hour of mating ends. These are many
new butterflies, and death is no longer to
be eyed by a young girl, perhaps twelve years
old, slyly, as though the future were a man's
sleeve or stride. I wonder so as not to end
dinner in a farmhouse. We sat at a low table.
Our host was dying but unaware, as she would

be murdered the next day in a distant city. There is an out-
side of language that is not silence. There is an outside of
God that is not isolation, a domestic animal teaching a dying
woman to hunt. A wound opens. A gate opens. Tendrils climb.

FROM

There Are Three

A Branch of the Discipline

The red forest is
eager to be seen.
The red fragrance
travels a great distance,
meaning nothing in
general, but in
particular fatal
and entirely personal.

The soul at present
matters less than
instinct, its
later instrument.
Of the 47 nesting
herons displaced
by recent storms,
47 died.

The red forest maintains
perfect silence, eager
to be seen without
distraction. In clear
heavens of destruction
it aborts the unspoken
words so easy to defy.
The soul is a nest.

The soul catches the wind
between numerals. Once
I was eager to remain outside
forever, and once I did.
The future bent
the boughs to breaking.
They cracked silently,
one last thing.

Overthrow

I.

On such a night, the stars could not consent to constellations.

My ambition was
at once to stop
dreaming and begin
to sleep, to make
a clear distinction
between the ache
of privation
and cold surfeits
of black sleep.

A calf defecating onto the sleeping head of another calf
instructed me the useless distinction intervening a desert
of joy a desert of defilement. It was no dream. On such a
night, the stars pour down soil through their names.

My ambition was
at once to stop
the river upstanding
the open sea refusing
all surfeits.

2.

Remember unequivocally the instance of mercy,
never prayer. The grammar makes deep channels
and useful islands, the overthrow of swimmers
recurring, undisguised. Mercy remains aloft.

Afterwards will
be nothing to pray.
The broad wake
of so many drowned,

weightless but heavy
with downdraft, did
not say words.

The sum of their pains in pain no more upon the world
undressed all sums. And into all such nakedness hurry
the prayerful, quick to flaw what does not make reply.

On such a night
I saw an earth
above the earth so
long as there was light
until it was gone.

3.

Two alone beside a park:
one is the art school.
Two alone and then a playfield:
one is my hotel.

When the light was gone and the grammar of the congregation
grew accustomed to darkness, only then could the renovation
of sums, nakedness and mercy excel the ocean.

Couples undress in their hotels.
One alone undresses in the art school.
A surplus of privation
renovates the sex of each
into the earth of all.

Night nevertheless. Consenting if amazed, I dreamed a dream
of flying, a haphazard innocence impossible to divide among
the agonies of surface and the soils of the unecstatic air.

Ambition is disgrace.
Although I could not pray,
I chose to pray badly.
Of course it was ugly.

4.

Ambition inquired,
are you the martyred
ocean or infrequent rain?
Of course it was ugly.

Of course my savior
was weathered by rain.
What remains of the crucifix
is a grinning spoon.

Very soon now the untethered reason of John Calvin
will roam at large in beautiful cities and kill men.

Undressed in a hotel
in Holland the naked vowels
in black and black pallor
copulate like seaways.

Undressed in the art school
in Amsterdam and inwardly
the martyr howls. She
is teeming inwardly.

An unlikely Puritan likewise howls for her.

5.

At dawn my nature,
remarkable bird
tethered amid predators,
alarmed my loving.

On such a morning
decline is lofty.
Teeming inwardly,
consenting to nothing,

the calf wakes,
ambition wakes,
the insensible swimmer
breaks the air.

Inspired is no way in.
Prayer and uniformity
are no way.
In each in daylight

a desert intervenes,
and then a dream divides
the night following
into white designs.

Upon Diagnosis

Being so fast, the things
of this world cling
always to excitement,
seldom or never
to one another.
Pathos is ravishment
by gravity. Myth is monsters
clinging to moments.

To the splendid encampment
Achilles summoned monsters.
Not one arrived, nor
plain nor particular.
Myth is the disappointment
of heroes. Nature
is likewise a disfigurement
of women and men.

I see a shadow meant
for someone else becoming
mine. I hear a blunt
inhuman sound becoming
sharply human. I want
attachment
to literally everything
elemental so everlasting.

Elegy

myself the other
winter even more
myself the other
still as obscure
a milk white one
a coal black one
winter even more

There Are Three

The moment advances
an illusion that high
sounds perish leaving
illusion free to survive.
This is silence.

An hour along
the groundless tangents
of a meadow is not wasted
until it ends. I feel
the world the less
the more it shows.
This is a picture.

My life disordered itself
amply in chronology
and voices of wolves.
No more voices!
This is a tune.

To the Lord Protector

I.

It is incredible
how cold, how far
from all feeling
the spur feels.

Me next. In the middle
way of scarecrow and
imagination, I do not
wonder. I do not open.

Against intelligible flame,
against the goad,
the craving for piety,
God established the body.

The shifting flaws of human permission made it move.

2.

Cruel to remain
in solace, such
a house whose
sound cannot consist
of humanness.

The table is
hazardous. The door
is accidental.
Loneliness never
welcomes echoes.

I taste it sharply.
As it dreams
to happen, sharp

I taste it.
I clash and conjecture.

A thing of stone is not a continuity.

3.

Many find immediate
rest and human things
exempt from harm.
Seeds and sparkles
all blaze again.

But even a famous
man may not
oblige jailers,
so wild a race
has superstition run.

If any two
tasted once
remedy for loneliness,
calamity remains.
Laws are imposed.

Cure of disease crept into the best part of human society.

4.

I trust to protect
tables, astronomy,
and the unconjugal
mind not to suffer.

Words declare
no expression.
Mind hangs off,
closing proportion.

Preposterous
to have made
provisions
while I dreamed.

Soul's lawful contentment is only the fountain.

5.

A discreet man
in wild affections
remains more alone.

More deeply rooted
in other burning
in rational burning

he honors himself
to understand himself
and be considered.

The least grain
is well enough.
Many are married.

God does not principally take care of such cattle.

6.

To end the question
men may often
borrow compulsion
from a snare.

Exhortation is angels.
Compulsion is devils.
One hides, one
bares the claws.

I saw the least sinew
of my body washed
and salted. I saw
it seeking.

The obscene evidence of the question never changed.

7. (Dedication)

This day will be
remarkable
or my last.
Like a beast,
I am content
and mutable,
perhaps free.

A few and easy
things, a few words
unearthed in season
revive the ruined
man on earth.
The effortless rainbow
deepens.

My author sang and was deep in her showing.

Extinction

usually unheard

        it is so common

needing only a few

        more words or one

success you cannot dispose of it

        by listening to it

and so a difference

        in cultures in the case of men

cannot dispose of it

        only changes the weeds

and emphasis

        of the cold wildflowers

living a few more days

Advent

The wind that shows a city
fills an iris, also
a heart suspended without wires
in the sparse lighting.

On a winter morning,
homelessness rides an impossible
animal into impossible vineyards.
The next wind shows a city

suspended in each vine, also
hanging the man.
If the hour had moved
without wires or the sparse

lighting above the wind,
none was hanged. Snow
fed the animals. Their eyes
we named for flowers also.

A Clasp

Below the shapeliness
of every hand
exposed in error
of the hand's strength
ache the usual
ligature and tendon
inflamed by injustice
made, allowed.

At Epiphany, hand-
made civil traffic
steals through town.
Hilarious and undemocratic
is every miracle. Ache
and error, ache and
correction strive as usual,
unshaped in the disguise of angels.

Scherzo

I.

Snowfall narrows the streets and sky.
Overnight, many fires changed the air
to something close and homely.
Light alone at the surface of light
sparkles, equable everywhere.
In the spree of men's eyes and calendars
duration appears white. The soul
of duration is white also.

Almost nothing
but sensations cross
the surface spree
of streets and sky.
Rousseau: "My
ideas are nothing but sensations now."
Many fires
change exactly so.

Even the smoke
of almost featureless houses
sustains
music of variation
beginning in my childhood
every cold morning.

Rousseau: "The earth
of my understanding
is alone."

Of equal loneliness
light sparkles
winter durations
like the death of souls,

having noted all such memorable flowers.

2.

A winter street
at an early hour
is not stranger.
It is something added.

My soul rejoices and goes.
Thoreau: "The snow is made by
enthusiasm. I see no sabbath."

Immersion or
approach, it
makes a difference.
Death apart or
memory alone, it
makes a difference.

Every morning, beginning in childhood,
the music of variation sustains
the equal loneliness of every soul.

I approached my father.
I was immersed in my father.
In the early hours of his death
hair all over my body was like snow.

Thoreau: "The dog explodes
his alphabet better
than savages."
I see no sabbath, only
a stranger returning.

Claudia returns with news
of the first flowers,
ever the same but lately
unimaginable,

ice taking the full measure of blaze.

3.

Noise of arrival
allows the winter
a little while longer
like a sieve like childhood.
Still early but unstill
the street grows wild.

Rousseau: "My hope
is in danger of starlings."

Something I trusted
apart from solitude
died with my father
o worse than lonely.

A savage making laces and dictionaries
explodes his alphabet.
More slowly, the first flowers
pronounce a duration, music in
danger of starlings, worse than lonely.

Rousseau: "My imagination is so
much noise." The full measure
of blaze, my soul's portion,
speeds the news.
I am death. And so are you.

Unimaginable music changing changes nothing.
Children arriving indoors early
from the snow with fists of flowers
imagine the world has changed, but only
music changes. The duration of flowers
is always smoke. My soul makes a fist and goes
apart among strangers, unequal to the least

movement of the lowest branches in the trees.

4.

At least upward, at least the earth cascades
into a sparrow's nest, becoming wide.
My soul has made a fist. The street has made
an imagination of flowers shrouded
in daylight. Riot and arrival move
low branch, higher branch, four elements and five.

Like a sieve or like childhood narrowing
into a father's death, the street is alive
all right, increasing all right, but not changing.
Nothing added music to the snow.

Thoreau: "To the innocent there are no
angels. Wrecks of meadows fill the coves."

Thoreau: "I saw a caterpillar crawling
on the snow. The past cannot be presented."

Thoreau: "I am not penitent. God prefers
I approach not penitent but forgetful."

My piety
nested a while.

At least earth if
no angel schemed for me.

Earth schemes apart.

An imagination of flowers shrouded in daylight
riots and arrives. Speed, my soul,
such news, and quiet my father. No further
music survives in snow. Unequal
winter becomes smoke cascading
into the street. It increases. Thoreau:
"God schemes for me." A further music
forgets the flowers even as they bloom.

5.

As pain
and delightedness contend in a sick child,
a scherzo of destiny and flowers
contends in the ground, in the least upward
narrowness of street and sky. It opposes
piety to outrage, penitence
to the sheer speed of human souls.

Rousseau: "In order to please my dog, I
made a plan. The better prayer is mine."

My soul is alive all right, but nothing
to do with me. The street is greener
since I began, no thanks to me, no thanks
to any sacrifice imagined or made.
Unimaginable changes nested a while
under cover of increase and then arose.
My father died. Claudia brought in flowers.
A scherzo of durations and departures
sped the news of worse than lonely-o.

Rousseau: "I let them yelp."

To hound by underhand,
honor and pulverize.
To pay homage,
proceed at haphazard.
The better prayer is also mine.

Beginning in childhood
light sparkled and flowers
fisted their beautiful
contentions without choice,

only pain and delightedness.

No Difference I Know They Are

more of a red heart

                the powder man wants

the red-hearted the poor wood

                     has the aspen any?

greater use give me

                   gladness which has never given place

give me names

                 for the rivers of Hell but none

for the rivers of Heaven

                      this day

there is no paint like the air

                      this day

is a godsend to the wasps

FROM

Arcady

Conforming to the Fashions of Eternity

Conforming to the fashions of eternity
I feel no conflict only one with prosperity

Wild work
Needs wilderness

A man far away in forgetfulness
Shuts my windows each one with apple trees

I accept their company

From far away in the north
Uproar risings inseparable
Now from apple blossoms
Roar at my windows

        And each is a real shrine
        And each is a real cup a dark one with blue insides

Wild work grows over humans real moss

Arcady Tombeau

Enter chain
A loop an
Hour between
Fades
Capped before
Having happened

New sums
Sons of clutch
Two canticles
Along a dew canal

Poe pays
What do you say
To virtue
Pal

Light Lily Lily Light Light Lily Light

Light lily lily light light lily light

Imagically
Lightli ly

Outline stones for the wind

All creatures come
To mind to oneness

Where I am formless   When I go back into
My breaking through   The ground the deep
Will be far greater   In me whence I came

Light lily lily light light lily light

Imagi
Cally
Lightli
Ly

Nature a Corner for Me

Nature a corner for me
There will be no room
For my portrait

Besides I have seen
Enough people and horses
And extraordinary fish

To dream like this
Was worth the trouble
Getting here

My other ideas
Seem premature
Like ghosts now

The most beautiful star
Is crossing me

Xenophanes

Let things
Be believed
Similar

If not for yellow honey
Figs far
Sweeter

He sees whole
Hears whole
Thinks

Always he remains
Said so
Laboring

Cows would make the forms of gods like cows
What men call Rainbow that too is a cloud

July 4th Blue Diamond

It is impossible
Not to suffer agonies
Of attachment the world
Is really so wonderful
The mountain stain
Of the grass deepens
The solo trumpeter
His anthem ended
Falls forward weeping
Into a woman's arms
The notes are eternal
Many stars shine down
Through the roman candles
More brightly because of his tears

Heraclitus

Arcady is the kingdom of child's play weeping

Arrow & bow life
Arrow & bow lyre

        The name of the bow is biography
        The arrow is death

ALL SUMMER LONG
Weeping it agrees with itself the same river
AND SARAH
Coming down the stairs

Sarah your real name agrees
The path up & the path down
One & the same

Staring into her empty hands like a philosopher
Sarah comes downstairs

The Stars Their Perfection

The stars their perfection
Uninvolved with perfection
Nearer

To me as the bedpost
Mistaken for Benjamin
My son sleepwalking

Nearly awake
To my mind
Shine because they move

Benjamin go away

I think there must be a place
In the soul for perfection
I think it moves around

And no mistake

Tooms 3

For enormous
The farm has a big father
Read Erasmus
No needs remain
Walking among the living
Who sometimes cry

Balloonhead
Standing to one side
By which I mean a man
Wearing a crown of long
Balloons in the air-
Port lavatory (this
Is Las Vegas) laughing
While only a few steps
Away a boy lay
On the tiles removing
Artificial legs
To shit comfortably
His father waiting
To lift him
Ignoring in such
Serenity the laughing man

Our souls
Almost the equals
Of our bodies
Love the world
And stay there
Sometimes crying

I know the breeze from the air vents
Moving the tall plants
(This is Las Vegas still
Still in the airport)
Is not the ghost of my sister
Come to say all's well

And place a hand upon my shoulder
Meaning surely I'm no animal
Mother & Father before us
Human too and the four of us
Together are souls in eternity
In such serenity
But I feel it

Come into the world
For enormous
Read Erasmus
Flower & leaf are the same crying
Loving the world
Busted robin looks at deathly magpie

Anaximander

Once a very short time
They lived a different
Kind of life a howling

Wilderness does not howl
It is the imagination of
The traveler that howls

And the mind in which
The valley and apples
Have failed cries out

For a very short time
With eternity no dif-
Ference between being

Possible and being actual
There is a different life

In the 24 Seasons'

for Claudia

In the 24 seasons'
Instant complexity
Nature teaches
Nor freedom no slavery

They are labors each
Immeasurable
As the alive clouds
Race apart

Find outrage
In mornings out of place
This morning divided
To equal eternities

To the earth of small shares
Work makes a way

Hymnal

Do not THI
          NK
Me
Mean
Spirited as the cars
               ARISE
Ahead of the hour
In the directions
All of them arise
Too beautiful
To beautiful shore
Or valley floor
Not mean spirited

But more frightened than before

Tooms 4

It is a great half world
We were
Not put here
To disturb a spider

We are puppets in the best sense
Panda
Calls from a telephone booth on a desert
Indian reservation to the casino to recover
Her silk jacket forgotten there

Puppets in the best sense
On television
The panda is restored to the wild and dies
On television
The murderer is restored to freedom and kills again

Truth and lies
Enjoy equal eternities

Panda proves it
I sleep on the couch of her approval

It is a great half world
I mourn
Puppeteer Shari Lewis
1933 – 98 old enough
(Just) to have been my mother
Dying the same day my real mother
Receives the same disease

Panda

40 years ago Shari Lewis made an ageless lamb
Today in lovemaking
I smell the sweet of my real mother's

Yellow roses cupped and drooping dead
Mother is on the airplane back to New York City
From Las Vegas where I live

Mourning and disturbance
Make lambs out of human hands alone
No strings

Anaxagoras

Of all our lives
Two
Are real this
One
Presently and a past
One
Not very far
Nothing
Like Arcady desolated

He meant a hateful allowance
A different sun and moon

The same Hell
Wherever
You start from

Just Having Owed

Just having owed
Regard to cross
These shears of snow
I am for all purposes
A walking tree

I'm sore
I move precautiously
Scoring a child-likeness
Subjecting dearest love to too-dear scrutiny
The snow stays good as new

Woods again
Make suitable windows
Simple squirrel
I see Eternity marked you before me

Elegy a Little

in memory of my sister, Roberta Dorothea, 1940 – 1995

Linoleum and half a dozen eggs
In 1960
        Many towered Ilium
A brand name and a shopping list too

Memory distinguishes all things from
Only nothing
          I was born and grew
Rooms stacked up into houses
A few trees (maples) weltered in their seasons
Wildly like sea birds in crude oil
                What amazes
Me now amazed me always but never
Often eyesight is prophetic instantly

Seeing broken eggs on the linoleum
In the kitchen 1960
I saw a broken lifetime further
On as I see now my happy sister

FROM

My Mojave

My Trip

I am looking at a smallpox vaccination scar
In a war movie on the arm
Of a young actor. He has just swum
Across a river somewhere in Normandy
Into the waiting arms of his rejoicing comrades.

Of course, the river's in California,
And the actor is dead now. Nevertheless,
This is the first of many hotels this trip,
And I find myself preferring wars
To smut on the networks,
Even as I find myself reading
The Pisan Cantos for the umpteenth time
Instead of the novel in my bag.
The poet helps me to the question:
Does anything remain of home at home?

Next day is no way of knowing,
And the day after is my favorite,
A small museum really perfect
And a good meal in the middle of it.
As I'm leaving,
I notice a donkey on a vase
Biting the arm of a young girl,
And outside on the steps
A silver fish head glistens beside a bottlecap.
Plenty remains.

The work of poetry is trust,
And under the aegis of trust
Nothing could be more effortless.
Hotels show movies.
Walking around even tired
I find my eyes find
Numberless good things
And my ears hear plenty of words
Offered for nothing over the traffic noise
As sharp as sparrows.

A day and a day, more rivers crossing me.
It really feels that way, I mean
I have changed places with geography,
And rivers and towns pass over me,
Showing their scars, finding their friends.
I like it best when poetry
Gleams or shows its teeth to a girl
Forever at just the right moment.
I think I could turn and live underneath the animals.
I could be a bottlecap.

Going to the airport going home,
I stop with my teacher, now my friend.
He buys me a good breakfast, berries and hotcakes.
We finish and, standing, I hear
One policeman saying to another
Over the newspaper in a yellow booth
"Do you know this word *regret*, Eddie?
What does it mean?"
Plenty of words over the traffic noise,
And nothing could be more effortless.
Catching a glimpse of eternity, even a poor one, says it all.

My Mojave

Sha-
Dow,
As of
A meteor
At mid-
Day: it goes
From there.

A perfect circle falls
Onto white imperfections.
(Consider the black road,
How it seems white the entire
Length of a sunshine day.)

Or I could say
Shadows and mirage
Compensate the world,
Completing its changes with no change.

In the morning after a storm,
We used brooms. Out front,
There was broken glass to collect.
In the backyard, the sand
Was covered with transparent wings.
The insects could not use them in the wind
And so abandoned them. Why
Hadn't the wings scattered? Why
Did they lie so stilly where they'd dropped?
It can only be the wind passed through them.

Jealous lover,
Your desire
Passes the same way.

And jealous earth,
There is a shadow you cannot keep
To yourself alone.

At midday,
My soul wants only to go
The black road which is the white road.
I'm not needed
Like wings in a storm,
And God is the storm.

Short Fantasia

The plane descending from an empty sky
Onto numberless real stars
Makes a change in Heaven, a new
Pattern for the ply of spirits on bodies.
We are here. Sounds press our bones down.
Someone standing recognizes someone else.
We have no insides. All the books
Are written on the steel beams of bridges.
Seeing the stars at my feet, I tie my shoes
With a brown leaf. I stand, and I read again
The story of Aeneas escaping the fires
And his wife's ghost. We shall meet again
At a tree outside the city. We shall make
New sounds and leave our throats in that place.

Just Leaving

At sunrise the high branches of the trees
Fill with sparkles, and wide seagulls screech
Hundreds of miles from any ocean.
The city breaks the street we climbed the night
Our son came. Late this afternoon, he and I
Will play there, covering ourselves with dust.
As I do every day and more than once,
I think of *The Iliad*. Terrible
In all ways, it remains a morning book
Open to the unused violence
Of early things. But later today, when Ben
Throws dust into my hair, I will look
To see Priam old and Achilles
Old equally, his killing done, his limbs loose.

Meadowork

American flowers pallid in a cloud
Showed pink until the shadows moved
And it was red morning, colored
After Christ's own heart.

        Beneath the shadows, something traveling,
        In the near distance, someone kissing a doorpost
        Cried aloud

PITYS
A girl's name.
Pan loved her
Because she walked like butterflies,
Shaking herself in the pines

            Beneath the shadows,
            In the near distance,
            Loud.

The trees were coming into shape, all shadow.
I was telling my son
A dead flower isn't the corpse of a flower

            Because long ago
            A bad king locked a shepherd
            In a cedarwood chest,
            And the bees flew
            In from the fields
            And fed the shepherd
            Flowers through the cracks.

Son, a dead flower isn't the corpse of a flower,
And at the end of the day, dusk
Will come like smoke around
And still not put out the roses.

The Government of Heaven

1.

One and soon
Another hummingbird
Alights very near

They do not stir
In the branches anymore
For a long time

This is really the world
In June 2000
Ours and mine

Needing all the same
The government of Heaven
So many other trees
Are filled with obscenities
Disappointed things
Naked as the bodies
I sometimes see instead
Of men and women

Something governs the hummingbird so well
She delights in stillness
Even moving she barely moves

Something fades my son's wet fingermark
From the warm stone

And then more obscenities

2.

Promises concealed
Are skin (this from Sir Walter Raleigh)
So full of rivers it carries sugar

Let Greeks be Greeks
And women what they are
Fences thrill at the view

I make no argument
I ache only for silence just one
With nothing to forgive

For years I have pictured it by a river
Secret to America and wholly American
A shore of pines and one of birches
Sunlight very fast and white in between

The people are like berries and no handmarks
They are carnations
The river bathes them white as sugar
And no handmarks
Breasts bow to where the water sparkles
Governor my heart stops

River of Mandate
Golden Age
But sunshine doesn't warm the stones
And there are no birds

3.

Completing the scene
Is a tree surrounded
By bones of horses
Slaughtered like sacrifices
Even these are white and clean

Beside the obscenities
Summer of 2000
Heat sharper than winter cold
Heat like murder

America seems an undersea without rivers

Kingfisher's secret name is Jack Iago

And as Charles Darwin good man
Born the very same day as Abraham Lincoln
Wrote "three species of tyrant-flycatchers
(Are) a form strictly American"

The fleshy sweetness comes and not a memory it really comes to me
As you might come to a booth in a swamp
Then a river might appear
And then the whole business of appearance would destroy politics
Giving absolute sovereignty to the love of God
For wild horses Greeks women and fences

Governor your handiwork stops and starts my heart
In the secret intervals may this country really move

4.

October 1, 2000 walking the dog
In deep shade I see 100 yds ahead
In bright sunlight a red clown hitchhiking
But of course it's a fireplug
I could never say the word
"Clown" I said "Keenoo"
Pointing at the circus parade
On the pediatrician's wallpaper
(Rest in peace Robert Lax
Circus poet died this past week)
The dog and I were startled then
By the chiding of a big crow
In the branches overhead

164

And we started walking again

The French have especially loved American Negroes
Mine is a French family
Caw
How I love you
How the government of Heaven
Rests this morning in a crow's mouth

And in truth there can be no greater reward
For doing well than to be enabled to do well

Actual photograph of entertainer

5.

Waters overplussed with pilgrim stutter
Make more wilderness
The woods outside and oceans in

My saintly Billy
They hung my saintly Billy

In the Las Vegas phonebooks whores
Listed as "entertainers" show
Their faces sometimes
"Actual photograph of entertainer"
My mind stutters obscenities with names naked as bodies

The plot is the stutter
Is why
The wild is why

As a child I was afraid of the mantis
Not afraid that it might hurt me but instead
I might by accident destroy one
The mantis was protected by laws
And police cars cruised our streets

Saintly Billy
(We could not watch the movie of *Billy Budd* death so inevitable in all
the actual faces)
We are corrupt as Europe
Eating one another as they do there—Thos. Jefferson

6.

Lord dear Governor God
The elections come very near now
And still in the heavy leaf fall
And on all the pretty young people
Walking avenues of the deep color
I conjure more precise obscenities
Cruelties really sad as all liberty
Is sad without worship

On March 7, 1835 at least Charles Darwin
Discovered the afterlife of Billy Budd
"It was the most laughable thing I ever heard. If the ship's crew had
been all captains, and no men, there could not have been a greater
uproar of orders. We afterwards found that the mate stuttered. I
suppose all hands were assisting him in giving his orders."

October 20, 2000 Iowa City
I go out and I feel that every step of mine
Spoils the rime across the grass

In the government of Heaven
The grass is truly higher than here
Stones are warm as a circus
The kingfisher's common name is Abraham Lincoln
My son leaves a mark on everything
A shore of pines and one of birches
Where my rough feet shall Thy smooth praises sing

To the Destroyers of Ballots

For his cancer
My dog drinks
A wild tea
Of fallen leaves
In standing water

But this morning
We found ice
And underneath it
Nothing to drink
Only brittle leaves

No birds today
Except hawks keeping
A brown watch
Over no prey
Man and dog

Picnic

The story of my life is untrue but not
Thanksgiving Day when the bee fell in the bottle.
All days take instruction from accident.
My wife opened the red wine in a good spot
We'd found as we were hiking along a dry
Creekbed. She filled our cups as I cut
Bread and apples. We saw the bee dive
Into the green bottleneck and start
To swim. Then we spoke about children and ways to move
An old piano north to where our nephews live.
We finished the wine, and the bee was still alive.
I tapped him onto the ground, and he walked off
Untangling antennae from wings and wine.
We hurried to reach the car while there was still daylight.

Sermon

20,000 feet above them
I remember them really
Cooing like birds in their small shirts
And their mother on the bus
Laughing loving them
Her own shirt no bigger than theirs

We must make ways
Passengers and paracletes
To land the airplanes
Between human souls and children
To rain down still alive
The sexual memory which invented

Transport and places each of us
Into shirts too small and wingspans
Impossible for human bodies
Laughing out of mothers' mouths
Making their way from childhood
Into 20,000 feet and more of sky

Nothing to do with pity
Everything to do with Heaven
An instance of motion not moved
But given by mouth and all the other skins
At risk at the mercy of operators
The way that logs love fires

For Thomas Traherne

The ground is tender with cold rain
Far and equally
Our coastlines grow younger
With tides
Beautiful winter
Not becoming spring today and not tomorrow
Has time to stay

Easter will be very late this year
Thirty years ago
I saw my church
All flowery
And snow
Melting in the hair of the procession
As tender as today

A sight above all festivals or praise
Is earth everywhere
And all things here
Becoming younger
Facing change
In the dark weather now like winter
Candling underground as rain

Prolegomena

I.

Always the last figurine,
Almost an afterthought,
The youngest shepherd
Is set down by the youngest child
At the edge of the nativity.
Far from the manger and well
Outside the yellowy circle
Of incandescent angels,
He looks away, watching,
It seems, for the stray mother
Of the dozy lamb on his shoulders.
Here, I would learn,
And not on the crucifix
Or on a glory of clouds,
Is the first image of the God-man
Jesus to come down to us.
In some museum or other,
The rough statuette of a boy
Continues now as then beginning
Centuries of worship and worry.
Virgil knew. And Virgil got it
From Theocritus as I got it
From figurines below a lighted tree.
And the earliest congregations knew it
Without asking. Giving thanks
Is later than a prayer.
And prayer is not yet.

2.

I had a dream the laws had legs
And arms and they were carrying pigs.
It looked like vengeance to me,
Out of touch with the tender confusions

And lamb-likeness of reality.

I speak to my poem now:
Tell me your dream.

Adjectival, cultless,
Ill-defined and filled
With animals, it marks
Me off. Before I was human,
I worshipped everything.
I knew the difference
Between two and three.
And one was a woman.

I tell my poem:
Three are heavy
And do not dance well.

Poem says:
A white umbrella
Is a slim foundation for festivals,

And any way you look at it, you are,
Like a heron on one leg, halfway to Jehovah.

3.

The beauties of the world advertise its poisons:
This dozen of strawberries,
These two letters remaining
Of a Greek inscription
Never to be deciphered.

We are among heroes,
But who they are
It is impossible to say
Until the poison works.

We came to a natural bridge and the air was instantly twenty degrees cooler. We walked on, and the walls of the valley began to sweat and to wear red flowers. The place became too beautiful to leave, and so we made an offering.

What can the inscription have described?
Telling is selling,
Even just two letters,
Very different from two birds
Hunting over the valley.

We made an offering, and a snake came out of its hole, and the birds killed it. As for describing it . . .

The beauties are falling away
In the shape of a heart unequally divided,
Animals to one side,
The Lord God Almighty on the other,
And me sitting in Missouri reading Dorothy not Wm Wordsworth.

4.

The little things of the woodland live unseen
At my soul's edge because the soul is alone
In the grass and loveliness, unwinding
Itself in their eyes where the edge moves.
I want to go to the invisible and see it.
In Greece, every dead hero was a snake.
They suffered their inspiration, and then Bromios,
God of sounds and voices, found them names.
Who am I to be seen without shouting?
What use is knowledge disappearing down a hole?
Come out and be killed, poem says.
You'll find company. Three ash trees
I saw beside a lake in late October.
One was bare. One was flame-red. The third
Smoldered still in summer green, and it was screaming.

5.

Imagination is the agony of meaning.
One by one, the lynxes are weeded out.
At sunrise, a white boy climbs
A heap of carcasses and sings.
Women climb and kill him.

Poem says:
A sudden sheen in the delectable mts
Means the birds are awake.
It's settled.

But I get tired all the same,
Just as the women got tired
Of plagues and became the Muses.
I think all the time of a man,
Dylan Thomas, tangled in the sharp branches
Of a photograph, unable to bear
The memory of Heaven a moment longer.

Compared to Heaven,
Music and peace are shit.
Sheep graze on magic.
Birds shine a light.
I mean to choose
Between a famine and a poison sunshine.
O good shepherd,
Magic me.

6.

Always the last to arrive,
The Orpheus, the hillside ploughman,
Shepherds me too.
Poem says:
He will be the death of me.
Heaven's heron starves, and while it starves
It glows.

Here's company.
They come to the stable; it is almost time.
For a last few moments, God is a wild thing
Or still a flower.
And then arrives a beautiful boy.
I see his wagon
Now in this now in that animal.

Bacchae

Earth make no mts more
But fires
And the grasses
To feed them.

Have you seen
The red grass
After an earthquake
Craze the wind?

O my soul
We are too deep in
The delectable mts
To see what comes.

Harvest

The god grows with us preparing
Answers to questions none will ask
Or only the winged beetle
In desert summer air
Too warm for anyone to breathe

Aversion then compulsion then
Children exchange childish blood
For coronets grown with God
It is cool enough to breathe now
It is autumn for the taking

In Christmas

They were miserable comforters
Cardinals the only birds remaining
In bare trees and abandoned nests
Exposed to everything
Their brightness often a stab
Of the grotesque
More than sweet persistence
I should have seen.

And I saw the mountains burning up and the rubbish
And the people trampling over their own food
In front yards and in parks and in school yards.
How is Christ to come
To fumes
And cold prayers
All fires wasted on harms and obscurities
The American famine?

2.

Heavenly man
I am scarce to go
And well to stand
In a disused place.

Miserable cardinals comfort
The broken seesaws
And me who wants no comfort
Only to believe.

3.

The stream is frozen because it is cold.
The leaves are black and tufted like sea-waves
Because of wind and ice.
Heavenly man
The toys of the disused places
The seesaws and cowardly birds
Afraid to fly from winters and fires
Welcome you.

You will famish us from words
And from crooks and underbarrows
And from owls and dragons at night
And from the horses snuffing up
Fat and full with judgment.
Send all away
Until your friends are alone with their famine
Every day because of today.

A New Abelard

God watch
I am in the basement of fog
And shall act
Between enthusiasm and dismay
I call attention
To your pile of hoard
The really beautiful
Like the Egyptian poem
This morning coming true
And you know I am not looking

2.

God eat our suffering
Out of which we churn butter
See
How troubles twin us
The white doe
Afraid
The National Bank
Afraid
Although the soul we have
Is love's doing

3.

Start right now
If you are a twig
Start now
Protest
Skins and skins of death
Offer you
Our life it is what we fight for

With sun
The only stain in it
Taking out pain which was not accurate

4.

This is porcelain ground
Walk on it
You are more steep
Now than we were
Struggle I suppose
However close
Your vision and ours
Handsome one
This ground is the continuing struggle
Loving it

5.

Season
Cello
Shield
Trio
Somewhere
There is alive
At this moment
Some new St Francis
Law of object of a leaf
If he is unleafed

6.

A man walking over snow
Makes his way painfully
To a wooden shed
The door nearly
Comes off in his hand

When he grasps the handle
Inside
Rotten machinery sparkles with the damp
The iron smell is warm
To Almighty God it is Christmas afternoon

7.

Twig white
Doe trio
With sun the only stain in it
We are a protest
Raised against ourselves
And God comes now
And God is alone in a leaf
And we are snow in the desert
Making a new sound

The Arts of Peace

Engraving of a bull's head
Is surrounded
By a water stain
Shaped exactly
Like a lion's head.

This on the cover
Of a library book
Virgil's *Georgics*
1940 translation
Made in Great Britain.

Draw your own conclusions.
Water does.
Sometimes books
Are true because of rain.

Given Days

The attacks were tall, and then they burned.
I'd been reading, and then it was time
To take our son to school before the mustangs,
As they do every day, fled
The schoolyard for quieter fields up high.

The news was far, then close.
Something had towered above the sky,
And now the sky was alone. At bedtime,
I began to read where I'd broken off:
Walt Whitman, a kosmos, of Manhattan the son . . .

Somewhere between, a little before dinner,
I'd gone out walking.
I passed the fat lady and her lovely daughter,
A three-year-old, on the stoop where they spend every day.
Between them was an orange with a face cut into it,
A tiny jack-o-lantern five weeks early.

A kosmos

Suspended in 1912, the Brooklyn Ferry resumes tomorrow,
And the sky reclaims its own,
And the river reclaims its own,
And we are the despised.

October 16, 2001

Strange new flight paths

chains of the smallest pearls

And glint of the Colorado

small so
chained so

YOU COULD IMAGINE A CHILD'S DOWNY WRIST

Where never before
Mist showed over water
To the east of our wings

YOU COULD SEE THE CHILD
(Village of Blue Diamond, Nevada)
RUNNING WITH MUSTANGS
Signs of the times, no, these are brighter, these are heavens and damn
all murderers.

October 22, 2001

I am angry (10/22

> *The house I was raised in*
> *Still my mother's alone house*
> *1022 Vincent Avenue, Bronx, New York*

With my dog for being angry
At Jack Spicer on the radio
Or afraid

LOOK THERE HE IS

Under the table with his diarrhea
And his bandanna covered with jack-o-lanterns

> *The house is falling away*
> *My father's death my sister's death the Halloween I was ill*
> *And doled out treats in my devil's suit to the healthy children*
> *And our turtle died under a Woolworth palm tree in a*
> *Woolworth pond*

"Believe the birds"
All's well now the dog's asleep now
In tough tender strophes.

October 30, 2001

All around the table
Words before bedtime—
Psalms from King James and some of the Wyatt translations;
A *Greensward*, author I cannot remember;
And tortoises, all those poems
By Lawrence, the best wisdom
Re sorrows and abasements, women and men.

WHERE IS THE REST, THE DEAREST PORTION OF MY FAMILY?
Safe at home.

> *In the morning, water*
> *Dowsed a white spider*
> *Out of my razor*
> *When I'd done*

(Our son, I hear, has covered the house in fake spiderwebs.)

Over the phone, the word is
Stay at home tomorrow, Halloween.
Anonymous tips from somewhere in Brooklyn,
Anthrax and explosions.

"There are no just wars."
Happy birthday, Ezra Pound.
Happy birthday, Claudia Keelan.

God help John Keats tomorrow.

Cake and icing on her lips
After dancing a little
Because of the new trees
(Palo verde and acacia)
And our roses thriving into November,
Claudia kisses me.

Flowers never spoil. *(They are doors to Heaven op. cit. D.H. Lawrence*
        "Bavarian Gentians"
Singers never age. *(They are doors to Heaven c.f. Walt Whitman*
        somewhere
On the television screen
Cross-legged before a wacky harmonium
Someone from England sings
To weeping firemen.

So, sometimes, flowers never spoil,
Even in the long days after
Lightning strikes the well.

                (I am far away writing this—
                Tell me, is there water?
                How are the trees?

November 30, 2001

A winter night in Salt Lake City

In a bright window	In the dripping bus shelter
Alone in tender display	A schoolgirl smiles far away
A stylist teases her own hair	Into her paperback *The Hobbit*

SOMEONE ELSEWHERE I'M THINKING

Comes ridiculous news
Disappeared remains
Of a hermaphroditic moose

Comes really sad news
Death of George Harrison
I remember impossibly elusive
The prettiest girl in our class
Loved him so

By first light
The snow falls heavily
And, I'm thinking,
More difficultly.
Someone elsewhere
Bringing my good shoes to the ceremony
Flies to meet me.
Every blessed thing is elusive.
All's muddled.
This must pass.

December 8, 2001

These sentiments grow hair, and wings too.
Just look at the drains, look at the clouds.
John Lennon's death turns 21 today, and one hour
From now, in the theater over there, the curtain
Rises on the blind kids' matinee: _The Nutcracker._

Comes terrible news: Shahid Ali dead
Who wept at my kitchen table for his mother dead
And balanced then every wild animal slain
In the mts of Kashmir on a silken thread.
He died blind. He was good news.

As I left my hotel this morning,
The television was still talking. It said
These: "like a weapon on its wings" and
"Like a housewife knows her eggbeater."

What do you make of _that?_ America   (Arcady)
Is a country of many faults without a flaw.
Why make similes? Why be blind? All we need is love.

In the theater over there,
Beautiful young bodies
Are dancing in total darkness,
And the darkness cannot touch them.

December 19, 2001

Mornings of the war that is no war but,
As the man said, new reasons for spitefulness.
All's paused. And inside of that another,
A pause between shepherds and kings.
Dead winter, and the sap is rising.
At the raffle in Blue Diamond, we won the palm tree,
And we drove it home in a wagon under white stars.

Began where?
A place in Brooklyn and the spine of a book
On a shelf—*Journey to the End of the Night*, a trip
I would believe myself taking, ending
In a child who'd traveled for me the whole time.
Mornings of the war are sex in a toilet.
Real sunrise rests today in darkest night
Under a palm tree scarcely visible.
It drinks myrrh direct from Heaven.
When it's full, look for a good day.

New Year

I catch the smell of fuel without peril,
And this morning the moon is enormously pale
Over the Spring Mountains. Someone's cooking
Breakfast outside on a big terrace,
And salt-smoke darkens the moon.
At New Year's nothing's transparent.
Disappearance equals increase, and emptiness
Rises or falls according to no pattern

Because there isn't any pattern yet.
Etc. Etc. Bring out the mustangs now,
And memory, and terror. A birth
Yesterday so near, today seems far.
Should old acquaintance be forgot, sing
Another. And Jesus Christ is the next thing.

New Poems

The Dead in Their Sleekness

Strange fame to be suddenly remembered.
Even in the pitch
                 dark if you go
Fast enough
             you cast a shadow
Darker than yourself.

Strange to have a heaven to myself
From a friend
          (Shahid Ali)
Died a month ago today.

I think of automobile tires in the rain.
I see the dark wheels turning the rain black,
Leaving a track of silver behind them
Fast as themselves . . .
The wheels are my friends.
And so are the dead in their sleekness
When I am with them . . .

Without difference neither roots nor origins,
When I am with them I feel
As if two clouds had imagined a mountain
Taller than the rest.

The trouble
Is difference.

I think of stags wading in India,
Thick fronds tangled onto their heads
Until they seem like mountains walking,
And then a tiger swims up out of nowhere.

in special,/In thin array

*Almost invariably it (the Sperm Whale) is all over obliquely crossed and
recrossed with numberless straight marks in thick array*

In the rain, the black wheels spin out silver.
It is like life and death and thick and thin,
Numberless until the tiger comes.
He is my friend.
He is the shade of me,
Faster than I am,
When the sun sets like the cut grass flying.

Clematis

The trees have disappeared from their boughs.
Between
Yellow roses and red roses clematis
Climbs our standing Buddhas now.

Lords, resound like a cornet band
Right across this mayhem.
Lords, assort the live from the dead shades,
And move the flowers near.

I was told
To make a garden and not to care.
Mindful
Of what I could not know of ant's wing
And detachment that aches deadly ache,
I made it, and I turned my back on it.
The ants crawled to me. Scent of flowers
Broke free of the vines and sweetened me.

Lords, your music comes through the back of my head.
Lords, your justice stripes me with tendrils of fat pollen.

Before and after itself, the garden minds me.
Here is an ant to guard the ant, and a vine
To cover the wall where the wind breaks it.
Here is a love governs death, and it turns me
Right round to the clematis and gives me
A yellow wing and a red wing.
I don't care what its name is,
And it cuts my name in a tree
Midway up into the boughs.

Zion

Suddenly copper roses glow on the deadwood.
I am these because I see them and also see
Abolition, the white smock on a girl
Eating an apple, looking down into
The valley, a small train steaming there.
I go to the uplands to join death,
And death welcomes me, shows me a trailhead,
Foot-tracks overfilled with standing water.
Man has never owned another man here.
Aglow in the shade hang apples free for the taking.
I'm saying that death is a little girl. The apple
There in her hand is God Almighty where the skin
Breaks to her teeth and spills my freedom all over
Sunlight turning deadwood coppery rose.

Conquest

Found a field mouse drowned in the swimming pool this morning . . .
Call him *Signa Winky* if I were writing
A children's book . . . I spoke aloud, softly, but out loud,
"Who made the iris to stand upright and walk with me
All my life, from house to house, from New York to Las Vegas,
Could recreate a mouse a good swimmer and he would live."
Or did the mouse fall dead already from the talons of a bird?
God did not make me. God is new creation.

In a dream last night,
I climbed a staircase made of fossils of flowers.
At the top was a little room with a bed,
And in the bed was an old man, lanky and sallow
And long-bearded. Cradled in his arms, appearing
To laugh even as he slept so deeply,
Lay a small boy, tousled, with no flaw.
He would awaken soon
And then create the universe.

It makes sense if you think of it.
As I was saying to my friend who made the iris only this morning . . .

Actually,
I have no friend, yet my
Experience of friendship is so real
I sometimes find myself speaking
To him out loud.

I could also pick up the phone.
There is a man in England, and I love to hear him say
The words "Felpham" and "cottage."
He too is real.

Poor pastor mouse,
This morning also
There was a frog swimming in the milk
And another one sitting on the edge of the bowl.
They must have been great pals.

Visions of the Daughters of Albion: A Screenplay

The bride of Heaven is Greer Garson.
In *Mrs. Miniver* God hears her
Breathing her white address into the emergency phone:
Starlings.

No help comes.

In the cinema of high shoulders and the feathered toque
Even help is helpless.
And I am a bird in the cheap seats,
Calling backwards through the generations
Of Wise and Foolish Virgins—
Roberta, Aunt Mildred, Mother,
Can you see? Here is a new hat for each of you.
It is going to be war-time now, time for feathers,
And Mars, they tell me, has never been so close
To our spectacular and black & white Earth
As it is tonight. This is the movie we've chosen.
Nothing can stop bombardment raining down
Upon the bride of Heaven in her white cottage, Starlings.

My Virtuous Pagan

As guide through intermittent hells,
And anything short of Heaven as I get older
Is Hell, smoke settled in a hollow, and the hollow
Myself in the deserts I truly love,
I'd choose that beautiful actor Jean Gabin.
You don't know what I'm talking about.
Or rather I should say that very soon
You'll never know what I'm talking about,
Because in a hundred years no one will be reading anymore.
Nobody will see the difference between black and white
Or open the smoky book that was the sun
Over rooftop laundry. *Le jour se leve.* The actor
Shows me a mouthful of doves and eyebeams.
Off we go, fronting hells between ourselves
And Heaven, which was a cigarette paper folded
Into the shape of a star. The star was the movies.
The paper was books. Bye-bye. Gabin's overcoat,
You should have seen it, was big as love first thing in the morning.

Vietnam Epic Treatment

It doesn't matter
A damn what's playing—
In the dead of winter
You go, days of 1978 –
79, and we went
Because the soldiers were beautiful
And doomed as Asian jungles
Kept afire Christ-like
In the hopeless war
I did not go to in the end
Because it ended.

The 20th century?
It was a war
Between peasants on the one side,
Hallucinations on the other.
A peasant is a fire that burns
But is not consumed.
His movie never ends.
It will be beautiful
Every winter of our lives, my love,
As Christ crushes fire into his wounds
And the wounds are a jungle.
Equally, no matter when their movies end,
Hallucinations destroy the destroyers.
That's all.
There has never been a President of the United States.

And the 21st century?
Hallucination vs. hallucination
In cold battle, in dubious battle,
No battle at all because the peasants
Have gone away far
Into the lost traveler's dream,
Into a passage from Homer,
A woodcutter's hillside
Peacetime superstition movie.

On a cold night, Hector.
On a cold night, Achilles.
Around the savage and the maniac
The woodcutter draws a ring of fire.
It burns all winter long.
He never tires of it
And for good reason:
Every face of the flames is doomed and beautiful;
Every spark that shoots out into the freezing air
Is God's truth
Given us all over again
In the bitter weather of men's
Hallucinations. There has never been
A President of the United States.
There has never been a just war.
There has never been any life
Beyond this circle of firelight
Until now if now is no dream but an Asia.

The Bishop's Wife

Sensing death on a man, the angels,
Whose only atmosphere is hope,
Depart into Heaven. And they do not return
Until it is Christmas somehow in another man
Or a tomb stands empty. Holly-time, or the time
Of lilies raised aloft in our processions.

Dying, we adventure the only time in our lives
Beyond angels. And beyond the movies too,
Because the movies are purest hope, the wishful
Thinking of men and women eager to delay
Michael's sword, Raphael's departure, Cary Grant's
Bitter relinquishment of Loretta Young to life on Earth.

Death is my only advantage, my step
Into the surprise of sunshine
After the matinee. Blind only a moment,
I find myself walking a clean street crowded
With all the beloved dead around me.
We are not make-believe, and God is one of us.

A Green Hill Far Away

I'm like you. There's a tree
Branches inside my eyelids.

Too, I am the loneliness pool-side
And sparkles where a boy's head breaks
The water's surface—midsummer,
Late afternoon at the motel, two hours
Until the ball game, Wednesday.

Was cleverness ever spared a broken heart
Because of cleverness? Always
Is there a younger and more beautiful
Upended semi-trailer truck?

Like you,
There is a tree,
But the love poetry
Of the old men,
Penitent and beflowered,
Does not chiefly address my concern, i.e.
The ugliness of my toes and penis
Because of one illness.
My darling, I'm sorry for that.

Patter, patter, un-
Betrayable patter,
A secret oar and petals
Do penitence.
Ulysses walks all summer
Through the astonishing heat,
Shaded by only one tree
Still inside his eyelids.
He lays his oar aside.
The lies begin.

The first movement of Elgar's cello concerto becomes,
With a little monkey business,
Theme music to *The Perry Mason Mysteries*.

When the entire boy steps out of the water, he just keeps sparkling.

Today is the day
The desert gives up its baseballs,
The day
Its blue-black butterflies and dragonflies
Uncover the real sun no one's ever seen.

The Celandine Creed

"There Is No Natural Religion."—William Blake

1.

Bright sun a broken
Carpenter's nail where the lake
And grass resurface
Is one surface, an apparition
Halfway to a state of mind,
My loneliness, whose guest
So rarely welcome, dearly
Forbidden is the Lord
Brightly spread across this lake
Now and burned over the new grass.

2.

The sun is a world. The light is what we see. And therefore
Nothing but the light is real. An American painter
Once said "I do not paint things; I paint the light around them."
His loneliness was perfect, a state of mind at true peace
With the facts. A poet says "I am not regional, I
Am local," and he too is at peace, knowing how mankind
Is the shadow merely of its entire surroundings,
Shadows themselves: blades of grass, drops of water, a bent nail.
We live in a halfway house best described as Paradise.
The dead painter clears our tables. The poet burns the trash
In a pit out back. These chores are done in eternity
As we are planning a journey: Helsinki, by way of
Palermo. The light around these cities is a laughter.
Film stars call it "love." In her particular windowframe,
Which is a perfect square of flame to the sun's circle
Going down into the lake, Dido calls it "Jesus Christ."

3.

Of nails in Tahiti
            (best also described as Paradise):
"they (the Tahitians) imagined they were a hard kind of plant.
Anxious for more, they divided the 1st parcel of nails ever received,
Carried part to the temple and deposited them on the altar;
The rest they planted in their gardens."

                        And of hard death in Paradise:
"*Pinihia*"
Ellis (*Polynesian Researches*, 1:310-311) describes the practice thus:
"The legs & arms were broken, round the feet and hands a kind of
fringe of ti-leaves was tied, a rope was tied around the neck, by which
the body was drawn up towards the branch of a tree, from which it
remained suspended; a small cord, attached to one of the feet, was
held in the hand of the exhibitor; by means of these cords the body
was drawn up and down: other dead bodies were placed on the ground
beneath, and beaten with the stalk of the cocoa-nut leaf, in the place of
drums; to the horrid music, thus produced, the suspended body was
made to move, for the mirth of thousands . . ."

At the burning window, Dido
Sees the shadows of one and two
And ten thousand caravels.

The entire lake is blackened
With black sails stitched together
Along seams of fire.

Jesus Christ

4.

Bright sun, nothing but the light is real.
I rub a broken nail between my fingers.
My hand is a boat. My mind is a net
Decked out in fairy lights by drops of water.
Grass grows from my head, etc.

You are in one bed, sleeping. I am in the other
Pretending to be asleep. Between us
The sun goes down among the caravels.

5.

Halfway to an apparition,
There are no stars tonight
But apples fall soft girdling brandywine.
It is God's loneliness. It is God's mind
Knowing He has yet to make this world
A world. For now, there is only sleep
And the pretense of sleep, a half-made Paradise.
But apples fall soft girdling brandywine.
I believe in one God, and He has never yet
Created me. But soon. It's the only way I can stand it,
Knowing I am not created yet, not born yet.
This is the absolute sovereignty of God I love, i.e.
That I do not exist and will be present
At the first creation of the world, the brandywine.

Landscape with Tityrus in Vermont

Is the shearing done?
Was it done well?
I remember the hillsides
As being real
Workplaces for gathering wool
From off the weeds.

Exactly the same are beautiful
Waitresses lounging in their dignity
For want of trade in terrible
Chinese restaurants.
I mean beauty
Is a discard of our too-late labor now.

So lately, many have settled in the remote places,
Umbria or Vermont or any place
The blankets tear at our skin
Because the wool is coarse and the news,
When it reaches us, reaches us, then
Starves at the doorstep.

War starves.
Word of corruption
Starves, and even
Things near to the heart—
My old dog dead
And burned and in a box
Beside my unopened mail—
Starve.

On the hillsides over there
In the wooly November snow,
Cow mounts cow, ewe mounts ewe.
News of the American empire
Blows into drifts against broken fences.

Io, I remember,
Was a cow,
And her father a river.
Corruption in Heaven
Made such hap.

If Andrew Marvell had had a typewriter,
If Wm Blake had had a cassette recorder,
If Walt Whitman had had a brace of healthy sons,
How the hillsides over there would melt and shine!

Nevertheless today an exceptional pine tree
Even in November
Did actually burst into berry-red root and branch.
Unprecedented things
Are massing at the edge of eyesight.
Their technology
Makes holiday and fresh hills
And strong new fires for new gathering.

Landscape: Coronado

Wrecked and painted
    Like the part of a shell
        A boy finds

And then somehow
    The boy lives
        A good life in the shell,

A house so close to the rocks
Was Heaven's adventure.

And we find the hotel a few blocks farther down.
In every room, the televisions are set to one station;
The same movie, *Some Like It Hot*, plays over and over again
Because it was made here.
And even earlier,
Baum found his image of Oz here.

An American tree transplanted from Germany (*baum*) via Kansas,
This is Oz? Was.

Over here a palm tree filled with broken kites.
Over there the ruins of a pelican my boy finds,
Heaven's adventure.
Overhead, bombers
Because the Alhambra is at war with Marilyn and the Wizard.
Revenge is served cold. Heaven,

Sick of hotels and architecture and Islam,
Slides beneath the sea.

In my boy's arms, the pelican
Droops like an unwieldy flower

Because death is that way,
And how do you put it down
Once you've lifted it?

The ocean is God's holiday from God.

Landscape with the Spirit of Kenneth Koch Presiding

Canary yellow metal window awning bulges with snow.
In the neighborhood of a hundred such,
Each is at all angles to every one, and behind one
The smallest room is my first familiar bed.
I dream about this because it was real
And has continued a long time without me,
Minding the changes without much changing,
Hearkening to disasters, remaining itself.

Over the radio comes news of James, brother of Jesus,
His ossuary unearthed at a construction site.
The good evidence will survive until it is sold or blown up.
But James is all right, still himself, dreaming of the snow
Which falls on the just and the unjust, on the savages and maniacs,
And on the woman who goes out of her way to save my best shirt
At the dry cleaners on the corner under an awning of its own,
Brick red in my dream, dripping with snow-melt in the New York
sunshine.

Landscape with Free Will and Predestination

Lay the angel deep into its bell.
Have you done it?
Have you done it well?

I meant to go forward
Over a landscape with volcano
And the birth of Christ.
But I didn't go:
An illness, my little son's,
And the interstate north of Redding, California
Closed by snow.

To observe and to reflect
Simultaneously, that
Would be godly.
A kitten darts into winter sunshine
And claws its shadow.
In a documentary film, a woman,
Being childless, wonders
"Who'll remember me?"
Who knows?
Creatures are volcanoes,
And yet many childless people go
Unforgotten in the birth of Christ.

I still mean to go forward, but instead
The near-divinity of the documentary filmmaker
(I've seen a picture of him—
He has a mild face)
Keeps me home.

Lady, wonder no more.
The innards of the earth are smooth, like
The shadows of mountains.
Lady, something is happening right now in a stable near a star.

Snow on the roads,
Illness inside of everyone,
Cannot stop it.

Deep in its bell, the angel
Plays rough, plays smooth.
Heaven is emptied and fills the earth.
Volcanoes empty the earth
Until everything is scorched and smooth.

Lady, God has given us a kitten
And a documentary,
And the glitter beneath the kitten's claws
Is a baby.

The Pennyweight Woods

I.

Change is change. Until I open
The curtain I can just imagine
A white leaf curled inside a green
And then a transparent one, deeper still.

It is my eye when I was a baby.
It was born and grows and flourishes still.
I leave it alone. If you really want something,
Go into a child's body and use your eyes.

I am terrified, though, by the loneliness of children,
Especially my own son's. It is like
The too-perfect perfection of apple blossoms
In a black & white movie. I open the curtain.

Pine woods. Not a blossom in sight. The trees
Are thin and numberless, sunlight showing through
Only as a blackness becoming blue
At the very tops of trees. Pine woods.

Cuculus cuculat, make peace with the birds,
But none with hatred. In the winter's cuckooing
(*Cuculat*) make no peace with anger, but stand
In line among the children waiting

To pitch pennies through the bars of a cell
In Birmingham Jail. Martin's cot
Is covered in wishes. *Cuculus.* I need to see you.
Perhaps you have some oracles outside.

What a wedge, what a beetle, what a catapult
Is an earnest man! By faithfulness alone faith
Is earned. Walking through the pine woods here in Alabama
I am not walking at all. I am simply

Handed from oracle to oracle.
My head is hands and feet. The Cumaean Sibyl
Meets Edward G. Robinson in a red house.
Outside, a red truck waits with its engine running.

Done to death. The earnest men are done to death,
And only then does the golden bough break
Into too-perfect blossom, black & white,
And then the loneliness of perfection makes peace.

Peace inevitable
Sad or cheering
Lets the beautiful
Laws prevail
The news is
Homemade
It is the attitude
Of expectation
A homemade Jesus
Expecting walls
Prove sweeter
Coming down
And in that case

Not changing is the most like changing of anything I know.

2.

Am I loving you rightly, son?
Edward G. Robinson had nothing
To learn but something to practice.

Save your soul, son.
The flowers at Beauvoir
So lurid in your color photography

Glow a different red than oracles
And old-time movies now.
Little of Dr. King remains

In living color. Our center
Is behind us. The way between us
Is over the mountain.

I see a green dust just beginning to fall between us
And to fall into the bars of sunlight in the pine woods.
What a catapult when Jesus is ahead of himself!
It is roots upended.
It is an engine gunned by God.
Go to your soul, son.

3.

Dot and carry one.

Once you were in an orchard
That darkened with every step you took.
To live better
And it can be done,
Dot and carry one.

Never mind the rats
In the house, son, cats
Will take good care of them.
The war is a rumor.
If you are to meet God,

Dot and carry one.

4.

Alabama skedaddles into the pine woods,
And who can blame her? In the pine woods
There are windows here and there, no dead walls,
And blossoms on the ground. They come
From somewhere, and you can find it, an orchard
That brightens every step the other side of these pines,

These pennyweight windows, and I never knew the sun
To be knocked down yet and dragged through the mud.
Handed from oracle to oracle, have you?

Or stops to remember, because remembering is a good thing too, like

Skates long ago
In Birmingham Jail
A new jackknife
We can wear
Old clothes there

Who would have guessed that jail
Is an apple tree, an orchard of one?
Alas, the United States Army! Who guessed?
If you know the taste of your own heart and like it,
Come into the woods to the red house
Whose windows explode from the walls and wash
Me clean.

My legs are stronger,
And that is all that ails me.
I send you this information
As I might the birth of a child.

5.

I say to the oracles, sweetness is in me,
And mine is the sugar to sweeten sugar with,
Like the birth of a child,
Like catapult and jackknife,
Like the syllables by which the cuckoo calls to deer,
Like the belling of deer,
Like the delicate sphinx of Edward G. Robinson,
Like the blink of an eye changing dust to apples,
Like pennies,
Like Birmingham Jail collapsing under the weight of pennies
When the golden bough breaks and oracles are ended,
Like remembering that remembering is a good thing too.

You will accordingly find an orchard enclosed with my shadow.
Now praise away until all is blue.

I ran into the woods to find the red house.
But what is the use of a house without
A planet to put it on? I mean, without Peace?
Until the armies disperse,
It is better to cook my food with broken glass
Than with fire.

The black & white cinema wants to know
Where have they taken our Lord?
The beetle asks the flowers at Beauvoir,
Where?

Change is change.
Here is my eye when I was a baby.
It is clean for you now
And for the rest of the family
Helping the sunshine over there.

Recent Titles from Alice James Books

Matadora, Sarah Gambito
In the Ghost-House Acquainted, Kevin Goodan
The Devotion Field, Claudia Keelan
Into Perfect Spheres Such Holes Are Pierced, Catherine Barnett
Goest, Cole Swensen
Night of a Thousand Blossoms, Frank X. Gaspar
Mister Goodbye Easter Island, Jon Woodward
The Devil's Garden, Adrian Matejka
The Wind, Master Cherry, the Wind, Larissa Szporluk
North True South Bright, Dan Beachy-Quick
My Mojave, Donald Revell
Granted, Mary Szybist
Sails the Wind Left Behind, Alessandra Lynch
Sea Gate, Jocelyn Emerson
An Ordinary Day, Xue Di
The Captain Lands in Paradise, Sarah Manguso
Ladder Music, Ellen Doré Watson
Self and Simulacra, Liz Waldner
Live Feed, Tom Thompson
The Chime, Cort Day
Utopic, Claudia Keelan
Pity the Bathtub Its Forced Embrace of the Human Form, Matthea Harvey
Isthmus, Alice Jones
The Arrival of the Future, B.H. Fairchild
The Kingdom of the Subjunctive, Suzanne Wise
Camera Lyrica, Amy Newman
How I Got Lost So Close to Home, Amy Dryansky
Zero Gravity, Eric Gamalinda
Fire & Flower, Laura Kasischke
The Groundnote, Janet Kaplan
An Ark of Sorts, Celia Gilbert
The Way Out, Lisa Sewell
The Art of the Lathe, B.H. Fairchild
Generation, Sharon Kraus
Journey Fruit, Kinereth Gensler
We Live in Bodies, Ellen Doré Watson

ALICE JAMES BOOKS has been publishing exclusively poetry since 1973. One of the few presses in the country that is run collectively, the cooperative selects manuscripts for publication through both regional and national annual competitions. New regional authors become active members of the cooperative, participating in the editorial decisions of the press. The press, which historically has placed an emphasis on publishing women poets, was named for Alice James, sister of William and Henry, whose fine journal and gift for writing went unrecognized within her lifetime.

TYPESET AND DESIGNED BY MIKE BURTON

PRINTED BY THOMSON-SHORE